Cover, Illustrations and Layout by
David Fitzgerald & Co. (Studio) Ltd.,
London, England.

Photographs :
Dr. V. Ang, pages 79, 96, 130
Dupla Aquaristik, page 49
B. Kahl, pages 12, 17, 85 top left, 91, 92 top, 93, 94
Dr. E. Schmidt Focke, pages 25, 42
Zoomedica Frickhinger, page 134 top left & bottom left.
All remaining photos by E. Schulze
First Edition, 1988
ISBN 974−87574−9−8

Published by Discus Limited,
21/152 Soi Tim Rungves, Bangchak,
Bangkok 10250, Thailand.

Printed by New Waitek Press Limited
383/1 Siphaya Road, Bangkok, Thailand.

DISCUS FISH

THE KING OF ALL AQUARIUM FISH

EBERHARD SCHULZE

DEDICATION

I dedicate this book to all those magnificent Discus fish which I have kept over the years and which have taught me so much, and so pleasurably, about looking after them.

ACKNOWLEGEMENTS

I should like to thank John Goulden and my son Peter for their willingness to go on running my business in my absence; and also my many friends whose support and help made it possible for me to plan and write this book. I also owe a great debt of gratitude to Mr. Kree Thammongkol for his kindness, to Haydn R. Williams and his wife Pensri, and to Les, Long and Micky, who kept the Mekhong flowing and made my stay in Thailand such a pleasant one. I should also like to thank Mr. R. Tanner of NCR Thailand, who supplied me with a word-processor and printer, which made the task of putting this book together so much easier.

CONTENTS

INTRODUCTION

The first Discus fish were imported into Europe more than 50 years ago. They had been collected in South America; and this source of supply has more recently been supplemented by fish bred in some of the countries of the Far East, such as Singapore, Hong Kong, Malaysia and Thailand. Japan, traditionally thought of as a fancy Goldfish or Koi producer, has now also joined the exclusive club of Discus fish fanciers. Imports from Japan are still not common, but, given the well-known thoroughness and the efficiency of the Japanese, an influx of Japanese-bred Discus fish can be confidently expected.

It is a sad and surprising fact, however, that even today more than 90% of the many thousands of imported Discus fish will be dead within a very short time of arrival — three months at the most.

Yet there is no reason why this should be so. As the great German Discus fish specialist, Dr. E. Schmidt-Focke, has said of rearing these fish: 'Anyone, even with little knowledge, but with plenty of dedication, is bound of succeed.'

And succeed we must. It has become obvious during the last few years that the quality specimens from South America are no longer to be found in the same numbers as before. Spectacular coloured or marked fish seem to have disappeared a long time ago. Of the better specimens, the majority seldom find their way to the ordinary dealers; they are usually reserved for the more well-known breeders. Because of this, Discus fish fanciers are assured of a continuous supply of nicely coloured and marked home-bred Discus fish.

The scarcity of good wild-caught specimens may in the end have its advantages. As there is no point in keeping or breeding badly coloured or marked fish, there will be little reason for exporters and importers to handle these fish and this should help to conserve the wild stocks.

We know what man has done in many parts of the world. We know that many tropical biotopes have already been destroyed by either cultivation, plantations or through overharvesting. Surely, we are duty-bound, for the sake of future generations, to call a halt to this kind of destruction. Then perhaps, in years to come, the beautiful, desirable specimens will again become available, instead of being lost for ever.

It is often said that Discus fish-keeping is very difficult: I believe that they are no more difficult to keep than many other varieties of tropical fish. They are, indeed, different: but once these differences are understood, any hobbyist with a little knowledge of water chemistry, the ability to test the water for certain substances and a keen eye for spotting trouble, should have no problems with keeping these fish alive, and even breeding them.

There is no single way of keeping Discus fish. This becomes very obvious from a glance at the many articles and books written about them; sometimes one even finds fundamental differences of opinion as to their general maintenance. This does not necessarily mean that the experts do not know their business, but rather that there are different ways of achieving the same results.

As a keeper, breeder and importer of these fish, I must have handled many thousands of them, from all recognized 'Discus fish countries', during the last 20 years. This book is the result, not only of these 20 years of collecting information about this beautiful fish, but also of many years of experience of sorting out other hobbyists' Discus fish problems. The aim of this book is to dispel the many fears a would-be Discus keeper is likely to have. I also hope to give to the more advanced hobbyist some scope for improvement, as well as helping to secure a future for these fish in our aquariums.

It is with sincere gratitude that I thank my many Discus-keeping friends all over the world for their information, help and support in putting this book together. To novices or aspiring fanatics in this hobby, I can only offer my 20 years of experience, and a promise of a great deal of pleasure in years to come: there is certainly no finer or more gratifying sight in the fish-keeping world than a breeding pair of Discus fish and their young.

Eberhard Schulze
Bangkok, Thailand
June 1987

HISTORY OF DISCUS FISH CLASSIFICATION

HECKEL DISCUS • BROWN DISCUS • BLUE DISCUS • GREEN DISCUS • PERUVIAN GREEN DISCUS • COLOMBIAN GREEN DISCUS

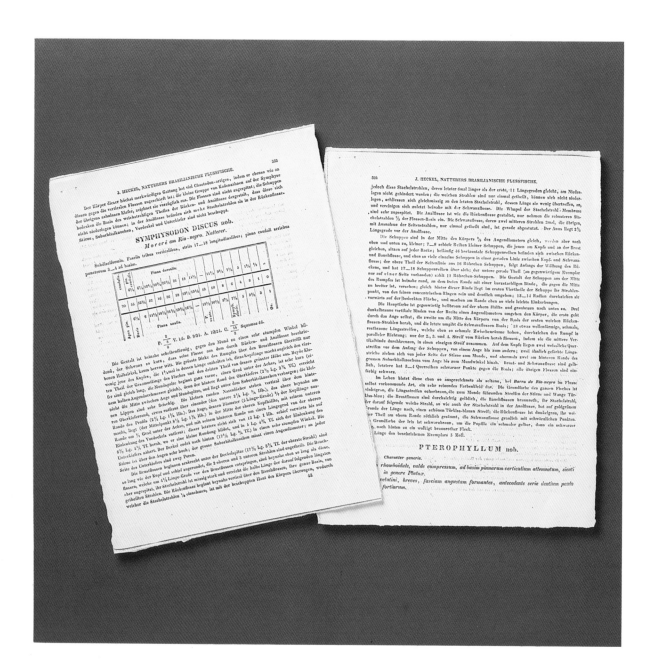

The first known scientific description of any Discus fish was made in 1840 by the Austrian ichthyologist Dr. Johann J. Heckel. Bibliographical details can be found in Pellegrin's monograph on the Discus family. Heckel's description was based on a single specimen, found in the Rio Negro amongst other catches. It was a comparatively young adult, measuring only 5 Zoll (approx. 75 mm). Even today, this type of Discus is sold all over the world under the name of *Symphysodon discus* HECKEL or Heckel Discus.

Discus fish were first introduced, in small numbers, to aquarists to Germany and the USA at the beginning of the 1930s. The first reports of the successful breeding of Discus fish came in the early part of 1935: Gustave Armbruster of Philadelphia succeeded in raising a number of fish to maturity, without the parents. The first real clue, however, to the breeding habits of Discus fish came when in 1949 W.T. Dodd of Portland, Oregon, reported that 'the babies were clinging to the sides of the parents.'

The latter part of the 1950s must be regarded as the period when Discus keeping in the full sense of the word really started. With more reliable and faster air-transport, these fish suddenly became regularly available. Breeding reports, with details of many of the difficulties, followed a few years later. By the late 1960s there were already serious hobbyists and breeders whose names were always mentioned in connection with Discus fish. It was not long afterwards that specialist shops and societies appeared, not only in Germany and the USA, but also in many other parts of the world.

Today, any would-be Discus fish keeper can find encouragement from the success stories appearing in many publications. A certain amount of effort will qualify him to join the exclusive club of aquarists who, through their determination and willingness to help one another, make the task of looking after the true King of the Aquarium an experience that will continue to be rewarding in the years to come. Once one is 'hooked' on Discus fish, no other fish will do.

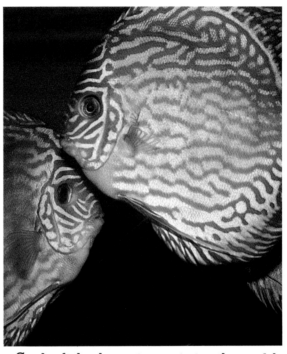

Such fish do not exist in the wild

Following Dr. Heckel's first description in 1840, several other semi-scientific papers were subsequently written about the Discus fish, but a completely revised classification of the genus *Symphysodon* was first undertaken in 1960, by the American ichthyologist Dr. Leonhard P. Schultz. Although this scientific classification is today generally accepted, it is still not totally recognized. According to Schultz, there are two species, with their sub-species:

(1) *Symphysodon discus* HECKEL, 1840
(Heckel Discus)
(2) *Symphysodon aequifasciata* with its sub-species: *Symphysodon aequifasciata axelrodi*
SCHULTZ, 1960 (Brown Discus)
Symphysodon aequifasciata haraldi
SCHULTZ, 1960 (Blue Discus)
Symphysodon aequifasciata
PELLEGRIN, 1903 (Green Discus)

Wild-caught Symphysodon aequifasciata axelrodi; the overall coloration of this Brown Discus fish is much 'redder' than usual.

In 1981 Dr. Warren E. Burgess submitted a description of a new sub-species:

Symphysodon discus willischwartzi
BURGESS, 1981

The main characteristic differentiating this new sub-species from *Symphysodon discus* HECKEL, 1840, is having 53 to 59 lateral scales, compared to 45 to 53. Apart from the greater number of scale rows, the new sub-species cannot really be distinguished in any other way from *Symphysodon discus* HECKEL, even though it is sometimes claimed that it shows a more intense coloration, especially the reds and blues. This new sub-species was named after the recently deceased owner of one of the largest tropical fish-exporting companies in Brazil, Willy Schwartz of Manaus.

Although many scientific or semi-scientific papers have been written about the Discus fish, it is still not easy to present a simple description. In a great many cases, specimen of Discus may share certain identical characteristics and yet the fish look different. I have often been proudly shown a supposed Green Discus, which in fact was nothing but the common Brown Discus.

The common names given to the different types of Discus have perhaps made it even more difficult to identify them. What is sometimes even harder, is to see the differences between a 'good'

of Discus fish which follows are based on the appearance that the various strains of the fish have in the wild state. Breeders have succeeded in producing tank-bred hybrid strains of Discus which present a different appearance and are described in another chapter.

HECKEL DISCUS

This is the most easily recognizable Discus fish, and quite often also the

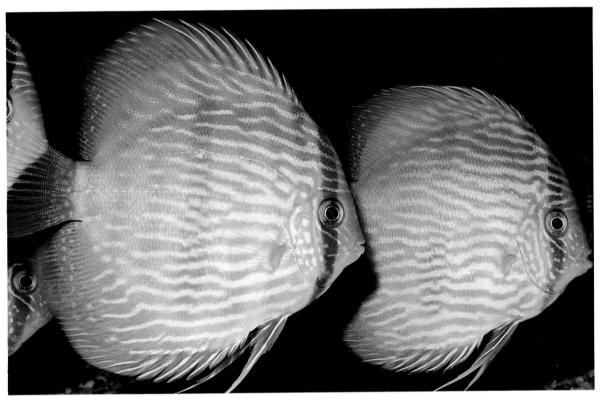

Heckel Discus fish.

Brown compared to a 'bad' Blue Discus.

If we accept that the descriptive common names of the Discus fish are, in fact, related not to their actual body coloration, but only to their markings, we shall then be able to recognize the different strains more easily.

A Brown Discus will have 'markings' only on its face and forehead; in a Blue Discus, these 'markings' will extend into the body; and a Green Discus will always have red spots.

It should be noted that the descriptions

largest fish in any wild catches. It has nine dark brown or black vertical bands, the first one through the eye, the last one through the base of the caudal fin. These are intense in colour, and always present. The fifth band is in the centre of the body: it is much wider than the other bands and also more intense in colour. The remaining six bands are very faint, and may not always be visible. A healthy and contented Heckel Discus will often also show these six band in reverse: that is, they actually become lighter than the body base-colour.

The colour of the body is more or less a silvery-brown, covered with up to 18 irregular horizontal lines. These lines will vary in intensity from a whitish blue to a light sky-blue. A stronger blue coloration covers the gill plates and forehead. A dark brown to black seam may separate the body from the dorsal and anal fins: these fins are often speckled with red and blue markings. The long ventral fins vary from orange to

the one most often kept by hobbyists about 10 to 15 years ago. Today it has had to make way for the more colourful turquoise strains developed in Germany, the USA or the Far East. Yet, wild — caught Brown Discus fish are often superior to some of the turquoise varieties available today. They still possess the true Discus fish characteristics which, very often, are no longer apparent in many of the tank-bred varieties. They still grow to a good size and retain their

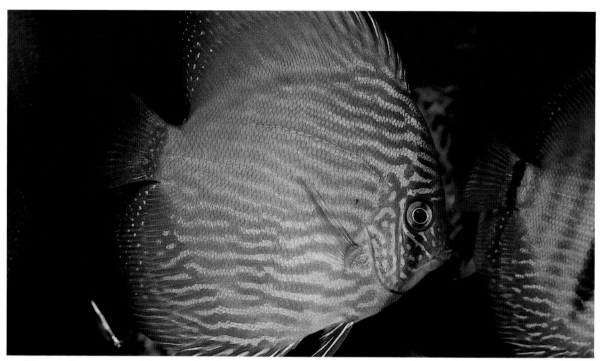

The coloration of these Heckel   Discus, Symphysodon discus willischwartzi, is more intense.

red, with one or two blue bands. The colour of the eyes can vary from light yellow, through orange, to bright red.

The Heckel Discus fish is probably also the best shaped Discus. Its shape is almost the perfect circle.

These fish are commonly known by any of these names: Heckel Discus, Real Discus, True Discus, Disc Cichlid, Rio Negro Discus or Pompador Fish.

BROWN DISCUS

The Brown or Common Discus fish was

shape; and very often they are not as difficult to manage as some of their more exotic brethren. But because they are just simple Browns, they have almost completely disappeared from the scene, valued, perhaps, only by some of the newcomers to the hobby.

The colour of the body varies from a golden brown to a dark brown. The dark brown or black vertical bands are always present, and are more or less of the same size and intensity in colour. Only a few blue lines cover the face and gill plates, and extend a little way into the body. A blue-black seam separates the body from the dorsal and anal fins: these fins have a few blue or red stripes. The tail fin is almost clear. The long ventral fins are dark brown, with some red or blue stripes. The colour of the eyes varies from pale yellow to dark red.

These fish are commonly known as Brown Discus, or Common Discus.

BLUE DISCUS

The colour of the body varies between a golden brown and a pale brown. The nine dark brown to black vertical bands are always present, but may be rather faint. The first band through the eye and the last band through the base of the caudal fin are somewhat stronger in colour than the remaining seven. The bands are of more or less the same size. The face, gill plates and forehead are covered with bluish horizontal lines: these lines also continue over the back into the dorsal fin, as well as into the anal fin. A blue-black seam separates the body from the fins. The dorsal and anal fins are often speckled with orange and blue dots. The long ventral fins are dark brown with red and blue stripes. The colour of the eyes varies from pale orange to bright red.

These fish are commonly known as Blue Discus, Haraldi Discus or Gipsy Discus.

There is also a more beautifully marked Blue Discus with strikingly blue horizontal lines covering the entire body as well as the fins, but otherwise identical to the Blue Discus.

These fish are always found in the Rio Purus or Lake Manacapuru, with *Symphysodon aequifasciata haraldi* and are, more often than not, dominant males. They are the most beautifully coloured and marked wild-caught Discus yet seen. Their name was given to them by the late Willy Schwartz of Manaus, Brazil. They are commonly known as Royal Blue Discus, or Blue Heckel Discus.

Wild-caught Symphysodon aequifasciata haraldi.

GREEN DISCUS

The basic body-colour of the Green Discus varies from a golden brown to an olive brown. The nine dark brown or black vertical bands are always present, but apart from the first one through the eye and the last one through the base of the caudal fin, they are hardly visible. The bands are more or less the same size.

The face, gill plates and forehead are covered with blue-green horizontal lines, which run from the forehead over the back into the dorsal fin. A seam like a black band separates the dorsal and anal fins from the body. The dorsal fin is marked with green or blue stripes. The anal fin is speckled with red dots. The dorsal fin is edged with a small narrow

orange to bright red: however, most Green Discus fish will have a bright red eye.

These fish are commonly known as Green Discus, Pellegrin Discus or Tefé Green Discus. Specimen in which the red spots cover the greater part of the body and form lines are today sold as Royal Green Discus.

This Schmidt-Focke bred Red Turquoise was one of the first imported into England; amongst a group of wild- caught Heckel Discus.

but solid band, red in colour. Red spots cover some of the body: in a good specimen, these spots will cover the entire body, and will often form horizontal lines. The long ventral fins are usually bright red with a touch of blue. The colour of the eyes can vary from yellow-

In the August 1986 edition of the American aquarium magazine *Tropical Fish Hobbyist*, Heiko Bleher reports on his search for a solid-coloured Green Discus fish, which he conducted in or around Lago Tefé at the end of 1985. He was convinced that such a fish must exist

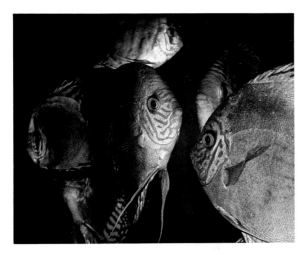

and could be found, simply because he knew that today's solid-coloured fish must be descended from solid-coloured ancestors.

To begin with, in the course of several diving attempts at various locations, he came across several of the known strains of Tefé Green Discus, as well as some with more intense coloration and markings.

Subsequently, he did, in fact, find what he was looking for, and so was able to prove the existence of a wild solid-coloured Green Discus fish.

The specimens he found were illuminated, sometimes with a blue iridescence, and sometimes with a phosphorescent emerald-green. Heiko Bleher states that these fish will be used by Dr. E. Schmidt-Focke as the basis for the development of new strains of Discus.

There are, of course, other colour variations amongst the wild-caught varieties. Although they must be considered as members of one or another of the above mentioned species or subspecies, there are two that deserve a separate mention.

PERUVIAN GREEN DISCUS

This fish was originally collected by Señor R. Wandurraga of Leticia in Colombia and from there distributed all over the world. Unfortunately, the number of specimens caught was never great, and when I visited him in 1977 very few fish of this kind were to be seen.

These fish were very similar to a Blue Discus, except that their overall body colour was a green-brown, with all nine vertical bands. The first, through the eye, and the last, through the base of the caudal fin, were more intense in colour. The eyes of the few specimens I saw were red. However, what made these fish different from any of the recognized varieties, was the overall speckled effect of their body-colour, showing red blue and green.

To my knowledge, these fish have not been seen in Europe for a very long time, even though one sometimes sees advertisements offering what appears to be fish of this colour strain.

COLOMBIAN GREEN DISCUS

This is yet another colour variety that is sometimes offered for sale. In 1977, I was the first to bring these fish from Señor Ivan Colorado, of Bogota, Colombia, to England. The overall colour of these fish was turquoise-green, and their eyes were bright red. These fish somewhat resembled a poorly coloured Turquoise Discus. Even though these fish retained their colour for a very long time, they never became a success with hobbyists, because of the apparent difficulties of keeping them.

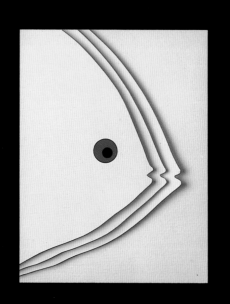

AMAZONAS: THE NATURAL HABITAT

The Discus fish are a South American species, and are found over a large area of the Amazon river and its many tributaries. They have, however, never been caught in the main streams of the rivers, but only where nature has created gently flowing backwaters, lakes or pools.

The rivers of the Amazon basin can be broadly divided into three types: the black-water rivers, the white-water rivers and the clear-water rivers.

The best known of the black-water rivers is the Rio Negro, which joins the Amazon at Manaus. The colour of the water is coffee-brown, but otherwise clear: the colour is the result of humic substances which have dissolved out of fallen trees and plants. Since the pH of these black-water rivers is usually very low, that is, the water tends to be very acidic, no Discus fish are to be found. There is also very little plant life.

In black-water rivers, Discus fish will usually be found only in the tributaries, in places where tangles of fallen tree-trunks with their branches and roots provide them with some shelter and security.

A white object in the water would be visible to a depth of about one metre. The carbonate and total hardness are not measurable with a drop-type of tester. The conductivity of the water can be anything between 5 to 25 μS, depending on the time of the year. The pH value also varies between 4 to 5.5, depending on the time of the year.

In the white-water rivers, the water is very turbid and almost opaque, but will clear in a glass collecting vessel, showing only a slight sediment. These rivers carry silt from the Andes right to the mouth of the Amazon river, and even into the Atlantic Ocean. The many published reports of water analysis of this type of water usually states that the conductivity is between 40 to 60 μS, with a pH just below 7. However, on a visit to Brazil, Colombia and Peru some years ago, I found that the conductivity of this type of water was up to 158 μS, and the pH 7.4. It is very likely that the water composition during the rainy season, when large areas are flooded and a number of minerals are released, is different from that of the dry season, when a great deal of rotting vegetation is bound to have an effect on the composition of the water. I have no doubt that the waters become softer and more acidic during the course of the Amazonian summer.

These tributaries to the larger rivers become smaller and smaller and suddenly are blocked with floating plants and fallen tree trunks.

In the clear-water rivers, the colour of the water is a light olive-green. It has the greatest visibility: a white object can still be seen at a depth of more than four metres. This water has the lowest conductivity, and a pH between 5 to 6.3.

Discus fish have been found over a very large area of the Amazon basin, chiefly in its tributaries. In the east, at the mouth of the Amazon near Balém, Brown Discus seem to be abundant, being caught in the tributaries, such as Rio Xingu. Further upstream, near the town

Discus fish collecting centre on the Amazon near Leticia, Colombia.

of Santarem at the estuary of the Rio Tapajos which is almost 25 km wide, a great number of Brown Discus fish as well as some Blue Discus fish have been caught. Further upstream, at the old rubber plantation town of Manaus, where the Rio Negro joins the Amazon, Heckel and Blue Discus have been found. Also near Manaus, in the area around Lake Manacapuru as well as in the lake itself, many Blue Discus as well as some very intensely coloured Royal Blue Discus have been caught.

Further upstream, the small town of Tefé has become known for the Discus which have been caught in that area, and which are considered by many to be the finest coloured fish among the wild catches. In that part of the Amazon where it forms the border between Brazil, Colombia and Peru, at Leticia, all colour strains have been collected except Heckel Discus. The Blue Discus from this part, however, do not seem to have the same intensity of colour as the Blue

Discus from around Lake Manacapuru. Across the border into Brazil, at Benjamin Constant, I collected not only Brown and Blue Discus, but also Colombian Green Discus which had an almost solid turquoise hue, as well as Colombian Green Discus with red spots on the body and fins.

North of the Amazon, in the rivers Urubú and Trombetas, both Heckel and Blue Discus have been found. South of the Amazon, in the river Abacaxis, the new sub-species *Symphysodon discus willischwartzi* was first collected. Further to the west, in the Rio Ipixuna, many Discus fish have been caught.

As we can see the Discus fish is distributed over a very great part of the Amazon. There must certainly be many other places where these fish can be found: however, these areas are still mostly virgin rain forest and many of them can only be reached by boat or small aeroplane. It is therefore likely that many of them will remain hidden.

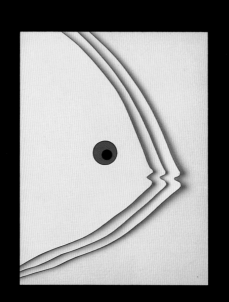

CATCHING DISCUS FISH

Many Discus fish locations are often situated in the depths of the virgin rain forest.

Catching Discus is very hard work. The chief areas where they are to be found are, as a rule, a long way from townships, or even villages: they are often situated in the depths of the virgin rain forest, in the backwaters of many of the tributaries of the larger rivers, and can only be reached by small boats. These backwaters are often blocked by clumps of floating plants and fallen trees. It very often happens that the engines of these small boats seize up, and have to be almost completely dismantled in order to free them from small tangled roots, before the journey can be continued.

Local fishermen usually know the spots where Discus fish can be found, and without their help one could never succeed. Although many excellent reports about the difficult task of catching fish in their natural habitat have appeared over the years in many fish-keeping magazines, I am including a short description for the sake of completeness.

Eleven months old Thai Turquoise Discus.

Once the area has been marked out, a fixed net is placed around it, to prevent the fish from escaping. The enclosed area is then cleared of all driftwood, roots and branches, by the local fishermen and their helpers. The nets are then slowly pulled in and the fish are trapped within it.

Even though this may take several hours, there is no guarantee that any Discus fish will be caught: if this is the case, a new spot must be sought, and the whole operation repeated. If the collector is in luck, the Discus he has caught are collected with a small hand-net, and put into collecting vessels. Very small fish are put back into the water.

Another way of catching Discus is with a powerful electric torch. This is always done at the darkest time of the night. Several catchers approach a chosen spot in a small boat (with the engine shut off, so as not to scare away the fish). The powerful torch is used to blind the fish momentarily; then they are netted with a hand-net, and immediately put into collecting vessels.

Later the Discus are transferred to larger vessels. The river water in which they are placed is changed very often; this process continues until the fish have been brought to their final destination at either a collecting point or a distribution point.

My own experience of catching Discus in South America was several years ago, when we tried to catch them by the torch method. That particular night seemed much darker than usual: there was no moon, and hardly any stars were visible. Although we spent many hours in the undergrowth of the still flooded banks, our yield of fish was very low. The noise from the forest in the stillness of the Amazonian night was sometimes quite frightening but the excitement of this experience was greater than any fear we might have felt during these hours. The lack of fish was probably explained by the still very high water-levels; although I had promised myself to revisit this part of the world, this has not yet happened.

Once caught, the fish are taken to one of the major collecting or distribution

Turquoise Discus with Heckel Discus characteristics. Dr.E. Schmidt-Focke was unable to raise many youngster from this 'difficult' pair. The female died shortly after this photograph was taken.

centres at Leticia, Manaus or Balém. There they are usually kept for several days, or even weeks, so that there will be time for them to recover from their long journey, and also time for any damage to heal that may be due to other fish, or to the ordeal of being caught and transported. Discus fish, unlike most other wild-caught fish, are given 'royal' treatment from the start, by being housed in large tanks or even tiled concrete ponds. Most other fish are normally kept just in netting suspended in water.

When the Discus fish have fully recovered, they are then packed in plastic-lined boxes for transportation. They used to be sent all over the world; nowadays, however, most of the South American Discus are sent to the USA, mainly because of the enormous increase in air-freight charges for live stock sent from Brazil or Colombia. It is now much more expensive to import the fish directly, than to have them flown from the USA. There are now very few direct imports, and this must be one of the main reasons why wild-caught Discus fish have become much more difficult to obtain in Europe then they used to be. Another reason, no doubt, is that the Japanese market has greatly expanded in recent years, and the exporters of Discus can command a much higher price in Japan than would be offered in Europe.

The great difficulties experienced in catching Discus fish, the often heavy losses that occur in sending these fish to the distribution centres, and the airlines' high handling costs, will always make the Discus fish a rather expensive creature.

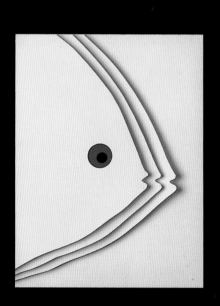

TANK-BRED VARIETIES

TURQUOISE DISCUS ● *RED TURQUOISE DISCUS*
BRILLIANT TURQUOISE DISCUS
RED DISCUS

Thai Brilliant Turquoise male, bred from German stock.

THE TURQUOISE DISCUS

The term 'Turquoise Discus' was first used by the American breeder Jack Wattley. Since then, many other breeders have developed their own strains of Turquoise Discus: notably Dr. E. Schmidt-Focke of West Germany. All Turquoise Discus are descended from wild-caught specimens from the Amazon, mainly Peruvian or Tefé Green and Royal Blue Discus. With selective breeding and hybridization over many years, we have today what must rank as one of the most beautifully coloured Discus: such fish are rarely found in the wild. But because of the long process of inbreeding in order to achieve the colour and other characteristics, many of these fish are not as strong as the wild-caught varieties. They seem to require a more precisely controlled environment; they are much more intolerant to toxins in the water resulting from pollution; their growth rate is often much slower; and many never achieve the size of a wild-caught specimen. Also, many seem to have lost their perfect circular Discus shape, and are much more elongated.

Such fish, even though they may possess all the required characteristics as far as colour is concerned, must nevertheless be rejected. A good specimen of Discus should not only show good coloration and markings, but should also grow to a good size, as well as being a good circular shape. Any fish not reaching this standard must be considered to be below par, and should certainly never be used for breeding.

In Europe, dedicated aquarists such as Dr. E. Schmidt-Focke, Pfarrer Schulten, Bernd Degen, all of West Germany, and perhaps to a somewhat lesser extent, Roy Skipper of Great Britain have devoted a great deal of time, not only to the propagation of the available strains, but also to hybridizing offspring; they have laid the foundation of strains of Turquoise Discus which today are greatly admired all over the world.

It would be unfair to reject all Turquoise Discus coming from the Far East as being below standard: however, at present most of these Discus, especially the ones from Singapore and Hong Kong, are of bad shape, because of the lack of ruthless selection of their breeding stock.

As I wrote some years ago (E. Schulze, *Today's Aquarium*, December 1985), the only way to improve the quality of the Far Eastern Discus is to refuse to accept any fish below a certain standard. This would eventually cause the Chinese fish-breeders to reconsider their notion that any fish that will breed is good, regardless of colour or shape.

There are, of course, breeders in the Far East who are capable of producing fine specimens: but they all started out with German-bred Discus. Well-known amongst this elite are Mr. Kree Thammongkol of Bangkok, Thailand, Mr. M. Smith of Hong Kong, and Mr. T. Tan of Manila, Philippines to mention just a few.

The hybrids, whether they originate in America, Germany or the Far East, can be put into 3 groups:

(1) where Turquoise, Turquoise/Blue or Turquoise/Green is the predominant colour;
(2) where Red is the predominant colour;
(3) where the whole body is more or less a single colour.

The fish in (1) are either marked with broken lines, dotted or pearled, or else are fully striated. The nine dark-brown to black vertical bands are always present but are hardly visible: the first band through the eye and the last band through the base of the caudal fin are always more conspicuous. The turquoise striation is seen on the face, the gill plates, and on the whole of the body: these lines also extend fully into the dorsal and anal fins. A small dark brown-red seam often separates the body from

Adolescent Schmidt-Focke bred Red Turquoise. The red striation is no longer as colourful as in earlier generations.

the fins. The dorsal fin is often speckled with small red and turquoise dots. The ventral fins are blue at the base and yellow at the end. The colour of the eyes varies from pale orange to bright red.

These fish are commonly known as Turquoise Discus, Turquoise/Blue Discus or Turquoise/Green Discus. When the fish are dotted or pearled, they are commonly known as Turquoise/Blue or Turquoise/Green Pearls.

The fish in (2) are either marked with broken lines, dotted or pearled, or are fully striated. The nine dark-brown to black vertical bands are always present but even harder to see than in (1). The red markings are more dominant than the base turquoise, turquoise/blue or turquoise/green body-colour: they are seen on the face, on the gill plates and on the whole of the body, and also extend fully into the dorsal and anal fins. A faint dark-brown seam separates the body from the fins. There is a narrow but strikingly red outer-edging on both the dorsal and the anal fins. The tail fin is dotted with both small dark-brown lines and red spots. The ventral fins vary from dark-brown to bright red, with small patches of turquoise. The colour of the eyes varies from yellow-orange to bright

red.

These fish are commonly known as Red/Turquoise or Turquoise X Red. When they are dotted or pearled, they are commonly known as Red Pearls.

The fish in (3) are a solid colour in either Turquoise, Turquoise/ Blue or Turquoise/Green. They may sometimes show faint spots on the base-colour. The nine dark-brown to black vertical bands are always present but are not visible except when the fish is disturbed. The forehead, face and gill plates show turquoise striation. The solid colour covers the whole of the body and also extends into the dorsal and anal fins. Small dark-brown markings cover the outer edge of both these fins. The ventral fins are blue, turquoise/blue or turquoise/green, with dark-brown to red stripes. The colour of the eyes varies from yellow-orange to bright red.

These fish are commonly known as Brilliant Turquoise Discus or Solid Turquoise Discus.

There are of course many other names commonly applied to Discus fish: Cobalt Blue, Powder Blue, Pineapple Discus etc. These fish are nothing more than variants of one or another of the strains already described. There are also some

Discus with extended fins, and these are offered for sale as Hi-fins: again, these fish differ from the basic colour strains only in having a rather larger dorsal and or anal fin than has so far been the norm.

One other colour strain, however, is often available to the hobbyists: the Red Discus. Genuine solid-red Discus fish do not exist. It is true that some fish show a lot more red coloration than others, but this coloration is only achieved through the use of certain kinds of hormones, and of other colour-inducing substances,

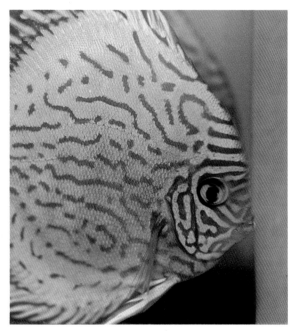

such as shrimp eggs and vitamins, in the fish's feed. These fish invariably originate in the Far East and are nothing but Brown or Blue Discus: the red colour usually disappears after a little while, when the feeding of these colour-inducing substances has ceased.

Amongst the many thousands of wild-caught Brown Discus there have been fish which showed a redder coloration

Dr. E. Schmidt-Focke and E. Schulze

than is normally seen. One such fish was caught by Heiko Bleher near the Brazil – Peru border in 1969. It was a bastard (hybrid) Brown Discus, *Symphysodon aequifasciata axelrodi* SCHULTZ, 1960. It was of a tomato-like colour with faint green stripes just on the forehead and fins. Heiko Bleher presented this fine female specimen to Dr. E. Schmidt-Focke, who was able to breed it with a wild-caught turquoise striated male with a brown base body-colour. The first brood developed into fast-growing fish with a red-brown base body-coloration. The turquoise markings appeared when the fish became sexually mature: broken in the males, and showing only in the dorsal and anal fins in the females. Although the red coloration was carried in the offspring, it was no longer of the same intensity as in the wild-caught

American Red Turquoise. Although a brilliant red eye, the body coloration became fainter with age.

female. With selective inbreeding, a more colourful second generation was achieved. After many years of breeding and selection, Dr. E. Schmidt-Focke was able to achieve the finest Red/Turquoise that has so far been seen. However, because of the continuous process of inbreeding, the fish have lost over the years not only size, but also their original intensity of red coloration.

I have seen many so-called Turquoise Discus fish in the Far East and especially in Thailand. Some had very faint colours, which can only have resulted from the continuous line-breeding or inbreeding of the strains. However, there is one breeder, whose fish I very much like, who several years ago started to breed Red/Turquoise and Brilliant Turquoise fish from original German stock: his fish seem to retain their red coloration even when the supply of one of the colour-inducing foods, the eggs of the freshwater shrimp *Macrobrachium rosenbergii* which contains a large proportion of xanthophyll, is withdrawn.

Experiments carried out by Pennock and Schulze in 1978 on *Symphysodon discus* HECKEL, with measured doses of paprika given daily in the food over a period of time, also increased the intensity of the red coloration. After a break in the administration of paprika, the increase in the red coloration became fainter and eventually completely disappeared. On repeating the experiment, it was found that the coloration could be increased again and maintained, so long as paprika was given as a daily food supplement. The same experiment was carried out by Schulze on *Symphysodon aequifasciata axelrodi* SCHULTZ in 1960, but no marked improvement of the red colour could be noticed.

Trace elements, especially iron, in the water will also increase and maintain the red coloration in Discus, and their use can only be encouraged.

The intensity of colour of all Discus fish greatly depends on their well-being. There is no doubt that the composition of the water the fish are kept in plays a decisive part, and so does the quality of the food.

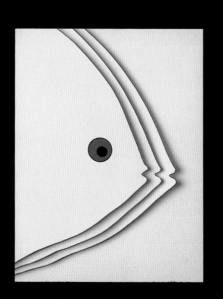

BUYING DISCUS FISH

BABY DISCUS FISH ● ADOLESCENT DISCUS FISH
ADULT DISCUS FISH ● BUYING
BREEDING PAIRS

When it comes to a first purchase of Discus, there are, in my experience, two sorts of hobbyists. The first sort, may have already been keeping other fish for some time; he may even understand some of the basic fish-keeping terms, such as 'water hardness' and 'pH values'; nevertheless, he is acting, basically, on impulse. He sees these fish at a shop or at a friend's house and insists on buying some, even though he and his aquarium are not quite ready to receive them. This 'impulse buyer' is usually the one who finds it more difficult to keep these fish alive for any length of time, and will in the end lose them all. He is also the one who will maintain that Discus-keeping is just too difficult; and although he may try it for a second or even a third time, he will finally give up and confess failure. Many prospective Discus keepers have trodden this path and have usually ended by going back to some of the more commoner and easier kinds of fish.

Quite often, though, the impulse hobbyist will have been infected by the Discus fish 'bug' — it is the only way to describe it — and he may finally become the second sort of hobbyist.

This is the sort who is determined to succeed. He has read most of the available specialist articles and books, and has a good understanding of water hardness, pH values, food requirements and maintenance: he lacks only practical experience. Hobbyists of this kind usually succeed. They stay with Discus fish for a very long time; and though they may try another specialist kind of fish, or even chance seawater fish, they always come back to Discus in the end.

There is no reason why one would begin Discus fish-keeping with adolescent fish, or even fully grown specimens, which cost a good deal more than younger fish. However, the novice should buy to begin with, a young, tank-bred fish approximately 5 cm in size, which will be at least 8 to 10 weeks old.

Younger and smaller Discus fish often do not respond well to the sudden stress of being moved. They may seem to be a good idea, because of their lower cost, but they are very difficult to rear and are really only a fish for hobbyists who are capable of giving them specialist attention. Because of the probable high losses, and replacement costs, the remaining fish will, in the end, have cost considerably more than the next size.

At the 5 cm size, the fish may already be showing a certain amount of colour, and if bought from an established and reliable dealer, should be in good general condition. The body must be a perfect Discus form; the contours of the head must blend smoothly into the dorsal fin. Fish with kinks in their heads will never outgrow them. The dorsal and anal fins must enhance the actual body, creating a complete circle. However, in so-called Hi-fin varieties the overall size is larger than the length of the fish, and gives the fish an imposing, majestic look.

The eyes must be small and red; yellow and orange eyes are acceptable, but can never give the fish the striking overall effect. Fish with large eyes must be rejected, since this is a clear indication that they have been stunted and will never catch up. Black, dull eyes often indicate a disease; when accompanied by listless behaviour, they often point to a seriously unsuitable environmental condition. Fish which are pinched above the eyes or just above the ventral fins must also be rejected. This is a sure sign of illness, usually of a internal parasitic nature. This condition is treatable, but the treatment is very time-consuming and the additional stress exerted on the fish by the medication often proves fatal. Discus fish with clear signs of illness or disease should, of course, never be bought under any circumstances.

Discus fish should be housed by themselves. They should never be kept with other species, especially Angel fish, which are carriers of many diseases to which the Discus fish are very suscep-

tible. When Discus fish and Angel fish are kept together, it is very common for the Discus to develop 'hole-in-the-head' disease shortly afterwards, while the Angel fish remain free of it, or at any rate, show no symptoms.

The fish must be 'friendly'. By this I mean that the Discus fish should soon return to the front pane of the aquarium, after initially scuttling away on someones approach. A gentle tapping on the front glass should certainly cause all the fish to gather there. Discus fish that are shy or given to hiding are always much more difficult to establish in a new environment. The seller of the Discus should also be prepared to demonstrate their willingness to take their food.

One other important point which the hobbyist must bear in mind before committing himself, is this: he must make sure that the Discus have not been fed live *tubifex* worms. Although these worms are considered by many to be an excellent food for fish, they always introduce infectious disease and other ailments into the aquarium. *Tubifex* worms may be safe in some parts of the world, but are a risk to Discus fish in Europe. Apart from the diseases they carry, they also often contain heavy metals, which always bring about the death of the fish.

The classic symptom of heavy-metal poisoning in Discus is a patchy silver-grey film on parts of the body: this in addition to the obvious signs of ill-health, such as dark body-colour, dull eyes and listless behaviour. No medication, to my knowledge, has ever saved a fish in this condition. Also, the commercially available live-food sterilization products do not seem to be able to deal with contamination by heavy metals. Discus fish that have been fed on live *tubifex* worms must be rejected.

Discus should never be kept in pairs unless they are known to be a true breeding pair. With only two fish in the aquarium, one will always be dominant, and will eventually make the other one's life a misery. The dominant fish will grow well, will make use of the whole of the aquarium and will take most of the food. Even if there is more than enough food, it will prevent the other fish from feeding, it will have the victim hiding under some cover, and if a whim takes him, will chase it all over the tank. Invariably, the persecuted fish will waste away and eventually die.

BABY DISCUS FISH

When six or even 10 small (2.5 cm) Discus fish are kept together, there will also be one more domineering than the rest, but because of the greater number, no single fish will really suffer. After all, Discus are a shoaling fish, and if kept together in large numbers, they are less trouble and grow into better specimens.

Another point to remember when first

Tank-bred Royal Blue Discus from Thailand.

choosing fish out of a number in an aquarium, is not to pick out all the somewhat larger or slightly more colourful ones, since they are usually all males. By taking them 'as they come' one has a better chance of having both sexes. At about five or six months, they will slowly

A group of young Thai-bred Royal Blue Discus. Although their markings can already be seen, with age, they will become much stronger.

start to show some of their colour and markings, and should have reached a size of about 6 to 7 cm.

If one started with 10 or more baby fish, this is also the time to separate out the smallest ones: they should be transferred to another aquarium and given special attention. Very soon they will have caught up in size. By the time they are sexually mature (this can vary from about 7 to 12 months with females and about 12 to 15 months with males), they will also have their full potential colour and markings. The colour may, of course, intensify somewhat over the next two years, but no great fundamental changes will be noticed.

Baby Discus fish will need to be fed very frequently. It would not be wrong to give them food at least 10 times a day, in very small quantities: not more than will be eaten up within one minute. Baby Discus always seem to be hungry. Sometimes it is advocated that Discus fish should be 'starved' for a day, so as to clean out their system, as it were. However, I feel that this should not be done to very young fish. Happy, healthy baby fish will eat almost anything at any time, and to stop feeding, even for just one day, will certainly interrupt their growing cycle.

ADOLESCENT DISCUS FISH

When buying adolescent (about 7 to 8 cm) fish, all that has been said about baby fish also applies. The adolescents may, however, prove not to be too sensitive to the change of the environment and will often settle down much more readily. I have always found that in matching their new environment to the one they were kept in, an identical pH value of the water is more important than the hardness of the water.

These fish do not start to feed as eagerly as baby fish; and if no 'settled in' Discus are available to encourage them, a few male Guppies will help. Although

this may sound odd, I have seen it done on many occasions in the Far East, and it always works. The male Guppies, which will swim continuously just below the surface of the water, will take any food that is given, and will make the Discus lose their shyness: they will usually start feeding within a very short time, when the male Guppies should be removed.

When buying five or six adolescent fish one should already have a very clear indication of their colours and markings. Special attention must be paid to the size of their eyes. Although not every strain of Discus fish has the same sized eye, if the eyes are over-large in proportion to the body, the fish are certainly stunted. This will remain with them and they will never catch up and grow into normal-sized adults.

If the fish are bought in one go out of the same aquarium, this almost guarantees a breeding pair. It will take another few months before the fish reach maturity, but there is then the satisfaction of watching them pairing off.

ADULT DISCUS FISH

The main advantage of buying adult fish is that right from the start one has fully grown fish, with all their colours and markings fully developed. They must not, however, have a ragged look about them, since this is a certain sign of old age. The fish must have a thick-set head with eyes that do not protrude. They must not have any 'pinching' either above the eyes or above the ventral fins.

Adult fish are often the most difficult to acclimatize in a new aquarium. They have been known to go without food for several weeks without showing any signs of deterioration. If no other 'settled in' Discus fish are available, the Guppy method will also prove successful, although it will take longer than with adolescent fish.

Many fanatical Discus fish fanciers have a 'sure' way of telling the sexes apart

At 16 weeks these fish already show good coloration. They were kept until adulthood in a fully planted and furnished aquarium.

in fully grown fish. They claim that the shape of the body, the intensity of the colour, the length of the finnage, the size of the eyes, the length of the ventral fins, the shape of the dorsal and anal fins, etc., etc., are indicators of sexes.

The truth is that a particular fish with any of the characteristics, i.e. longer ventral or dorsal fins, may turn out to be a male: but the chances are equally good that it will be found to be a female.

I should like to put in a claim for my own way of sexing Discus fish, which is based on more than 20 years of keeping them: although it has never proved to be 100% successful it has always shown a 70% success rate, that is to say, two correct identifications out of three.

I have always found that the females are more rounded in shape, and have a 'sweeter' look about them; and that the males are somewhat more 'bullish' in

their appearance, with a slightly more elongated body.

Another way to sex Discus fish with considerable accuracy, but again without 100% assurance, is either to feed them very heavily with a high-fibre food such as freeze-dried *tubifex* worms or to move them into another aquarium with a slightly different water condition and temperature. This will often cause the breeding tubes to project from the body for just a short time, but long enough, as a rule, to show a difference between the sexes.

There is, in fact, no accurate way of sexing Discus fish, except by the size and shape of their breeding tubes. In the males, the tube will be smaller and shorter and will come to a point; while in the females, the tube will be thicker, will project further from the body, and will be blunt.

BUYING BREEDING PAIRS

By buying a breeding pair, the problem of sexing is, of course, avoided. What is lost, however, is the knowledge and experience to be gained from rearing young fish to adulthood.

Good breeding pairs are seldom offered for sale, because a hobbyist who owns such a pair will generally prefer to keep them. By selling their offspring, he will have funds to help him to keep up his hobby. There is never any difficulty in disposing of young fish: the advertisements in all the fishkeeping magazines show that there is a ready market.

One should therefore be cautious in buying a breeding pair. The first thing to make sure of is that the fish are actually capable, not only of spawning, but also of rearing their young. It is useless to buy a pair which spawns but then eats the eggs or the newly hatched larvae on every occasion. Having myself bought many such pairs, I now always insist on photographic proof that the fish are indeed capable of raising up youngsters.

A good breeding pair of Discus fish should be from the same strain and of more or less the same size, and should behave very gently towards each other. They should not fight at all, except perhaps a tender nudge once in a while. Mouth-to-mouth fighting in a breeding pair will always be followed later in quarrelling over the eggs or larvae, with the result that the young are eaten. A good breeding pair should also not hide when any maintenance is carried out on the aquarium, or when the breeding substrate is approached with the hand: it should completely ignore the outside world.

Breeding pairs will react in two different ways to being moved. Either they will settle down very quickly, and

because of the often slightly different water conditions, will start to look for a new breeding site, and start spawning within a few days; or they will go completely to pieces, and stop spawning for a considerable length of time. In this case, the keeper is advised to introduce some other fish into the aquarium, preferably a shoal of youngsters, as this will keep fights from breaking out: with adolescent or other adult fish, there is likely to be constant fighting.

Buying Discus fish is a matter of trust and they should therefore be bought from one of the specialist dealers. Although the fish may seem initially somewhat more expensive, they are more likely to have had the correct care. They will probably have been kept in a more suitable type of water, they will have

been fed on a variety of suitable foods, and in general will have been given specialist attention.

Also, when buying from a specialist dealer the hobbyist can be sure that the fish he has bought will turn out in the end to be what he was offered. Baby Discus fish almost all look the same: but if he is paying for a fish of the turquoise variety, he should feel confident that a Turquoise Discus fish will be swimming in his aquarium a few months later.

It has been quite fashionable of late for almost every aquarium shop to have at least one aquarium with Discus fish on display, but usually these fish are in a very sorry state. Discus are a specialist fish, needing special care, which they are likely to get only from one of the specialist dealers.

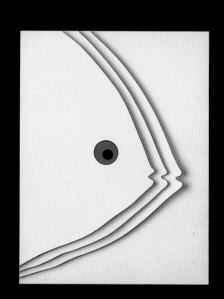

ACCLIMATIZATION

Discus fish have to be acclimatized very carefully to their new aquarium. The common procedure is to float the plastic bag containing the fish on the surface of the water for about half an hour. If the bag is not paper-lined, it is advisable to turn off the aquarium lights so as not to startle the fish. The lights should be turned off, in any case, once the fish are released into the water. During this initial floating of the bag, small quantities of the aquarium water must be added to the bag; within half an hour, the temperature, hardness and pH value of the water in the bag should be the same as in the aquarium. The fish or fishes should then be carefully released.

If the fish have had a long distance to travel, and the water in the bag has had time to become very cold, it is best to introduce them into cool water to begin with. The temperature of the aquarium water, with the fish inside, should then be raised gradually, by means of the heater or thermostat: and this should take several hours.

I have on occasion received Discus from abroad, in water the temperature of which was as low as 20°C. To have tried to acclimatize the fish to a temperature of 30°C within half an hour would almost certainly have proved fatal to them. The principle to follow is: the lower the temperature of the carrying bag, the longer the period of acclimatization should be.

The method I prefer also abides by this principle, but is carried out differently. The bag containing the fish is put in a small bucket, which is then placed in a 25-litre plastic container or small aquarium. Water from the main aquarium is slowly dripped into the bag through a small-bore clamped airline until it overflows. Once there is enough water in the bucket for the fish to swim upright, the fish are carefully let out into the bucket. Water from the tank continues to trickle into the bucket; and as soon as there are several centimetres of water in

the second vessel, enough to support the fish, they are released into the outer vessel. The fish are then caught with a hand-net and put into the main aquarium. This method uses a larger volume of water, assuring a better mix, and seems much less stressful to the fish as their reaction and behaviour clearly shows.

Bags are floated in a pool of Water.

A Larger volume of water assuring a better mix.

Baby Discus are much easier to acclimatize than adult fish. Adult Discus will often lie flat on the bottom of the aquarium for a while, with their eyes bulging, and cause the uninitiated keeper great alarm. There is really no need for anxiety, since the fish will regain its normal position within an hour or so.

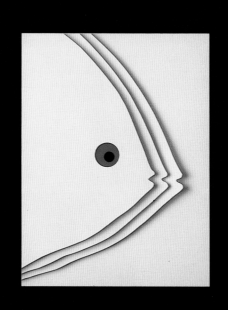

EQUIPMENT

THE AQUARIUM ● ALL-GLASS AQUARIUM
● THE FRAMED AQUARIUM ●
● POSITION OF AQUARIUM ●
HEATERS AND THERMOSTATS ● LIGHTING
● ULTRA-VIOLET RADIATION ● OZONE ●
THE OXYDATOR ● FILTRATION ●
UNDERGRAVEL OR SUBGRAVEL FILTERS ●
AIR-OPERATED INTERNAL FILTERS ●
POWER-OPERATED INTERNAL FILTERS ●
EXTERNAL POWER FILTERS ● TRICKLE
FILTERS ● SYSTEM FILTERS ● FILTERING
MATERIALS ● MECHANICAL FILTERS ●
CHEMICAL FILTERS ● ION EXCHANGE
RESINS ● BIOLOGICAL FILTERS

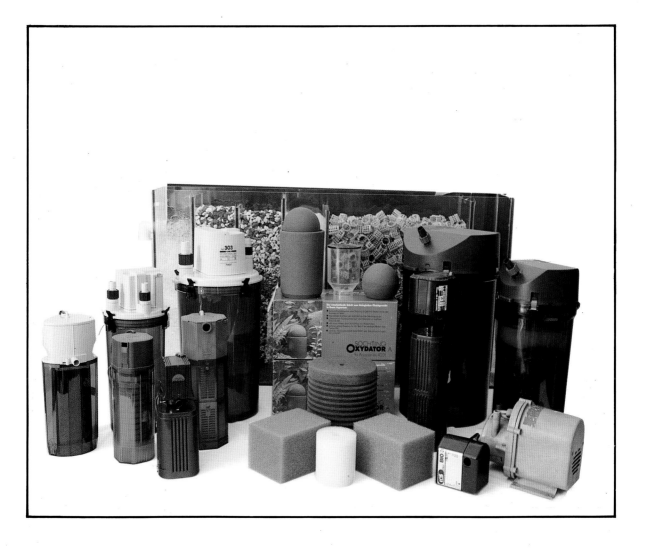

Very often not enough thought is given to providing the right equipment, with the result that one's first attempt at Discus-keeping is doomed to failure before it has even started. It is not good enough to use any old tank one happens to have. As good Discus fish are still not common, and cost rather more than other fish, it is obvious that the equipment used to maintain them should be reliable and of good quality.

THE AQUARIUM

With modern glazing techniques, aquariums of almost any size or shape can be contructed. The most important considerations about the size and shape of the aquarium must be: a) that it should be easy to maintain; and b) that it should contain the right volume of water for the fish.

The type of tank that is chosen will also depend on the setting in which it is to be placed. An all-glass type of aquarium often looks out of place in an elegant sitting room; on the other hand, a super-finished framed aquarium is hardly needed in a fish house.

THE ALL-GLASS AQUARIUM

The all-glass type of aquarium must be made with the right thickness of glass. A tank made of glass that is too thin, or even second-hand glass is likely to bring disaster, possibly resulting in the total loss of all the fish.

The silicone sealant used should be of the coloured variety — either black, brown or beige, since these sealants have proved to be much longer lasting. Clear or transparent silicone sealants are more readily destroyed by some of the chemicals used for the treatment of the fish, as well as by algae. The panes of the glass should not touch each other, but should be separated by an expansion joint at least a few millimetres thick to take the

stress exerted on the glass, either by internal water pressure or by slightly uneven positioning. The joints must be clean: an aquarium with smears or bubbles in the sealant will give trouble after a while. The all-glass aquarium must have one or several cross-bars at the top so that the aquarium will retain its shape when filled with water. There should also be one or two cut-outs in the bracing at the top, to take the tubing from the filtering system, as well as the cable from the heater or thermostat.

An all-glass aquarium build using the right thickness of new glass, with polished edges, with an even and clean seal of a coloured silicone sealant, should last practically for ever, and should prove to be trouble free.

THE FRAMED AQUARIUM

With the framed aquarium, there is more restriction as to shape. Although corner tanks, or even hexagonal or octagonal ones are possible, their enormous cost usually makes them impracticable. A framed aquarium is really just an all-glass aquarium, with a metal frame, usually alluminium, to give additional strength. Though such aquariums are generally made to a higher standard than the cheaper all-glass ones, it is still necessary to make sure that the glass is of the correct thickness, and that the silicone sealant is of the coloured sort with a clean and bubble-free joint. A metal cross-bar makes the aquarium retain its shape when it is filled with water.

There is another type of framed aquarium which is greatly liked by hobbyists: it has a metal frame only at the top and the bottom of the aquarium, leaving the four vertical edges free. The glass at these edges is stuck together with a coloured silicone sealant, giving a slightly more uninterrupted view into the aquarium.

The chief advantages of the framed aquarium is that it is generally more strongly constructed than the all-glass aquarium. Because of the frame, a more closely-fitting type of cover can be used, which will take the light fitting and other accessories, and give the tank a more attractive appearance which should suit any sort of sitting room.

The size of the aquarium should be determined not only by the space available or the number of fish to be housed, but also by the need for ease of maintenance. Although a huge aquarium, whose size can be measured in metres, may look impressive, it is bound to be very difficult to look after. To be comfortable, the height and depth should generally be not more than about 60 cm. In an aquarium of this size, it is easy to reach into all the corners. Oversized tanks can create difficulties in cases when a sudden illness amongst the fish needs attention, or when for some reason, the water needs changing.

A section of a 200 aquarium Discus fish breeding installation in Bangkok, Thailand.

It is probably impossible to determine what the ideal size of an aquarium for Discus fish should be. Much has been written on this subject, but no conclusion has been arrived at. It probably comes down to a question of personal preference.

However, a tank measuring 130 x 60 x 60 cm (holding about 450 litres of water) would probably come close to the ideal for rearing a number of youngsters or for

keeping adolescent or adult fish. This height and depth should certainly offer the Discus a feeling of security which will help them to settle down quickly and easily.

A tank measuring 50 x 50 x 50 cm (holding about 120 litres of water) is certainly big enough for one breeding pair. Such tanks are often used by breeders in the Far East, as well as in Germany. Larger breeding tanks are always more difficult to service; also, in a large volume of water, the amount of food required by the baby fish will quickly cause pollution, because it will rapidly be dispersed.

POSITION OF AQUARIUM

A great deal has been written about the position of the tank. It is usually asserted that Discus should be housed in an aquarium away from noise, stairways and doorways. The vibration caused by people opening and closing doors or walking up and down the stairs is said to make the fish jumpy and slow to settle down. I have always found, on the contrary, that if there is a certain amount of movement and even noise around the aquarium, the Discus very soon become accustomed to it as a normal feature of their life. Fish kept like this are always less nervous than fish kept in an isolated room or a quiet part of the house, which usually take flight at the least noise or movement, and reappear only when the coast is clear.

There is something fundamentally wrong with any Discus fish aquarium where the keeper is afraid to approach the fish, in case he startles them: and steps should be taken to put this right, usually, it is only a matter of re-positioning the aquarium in this particular situation; and after a little while the fish will behave less nervously. Not only will the keeper have more pleasure in looking after them, but they will also be friendlier, and display better colours.

HEATERS AND THERMOSTATS

As Discus fish require water of a higher temperature than most other tropical fish, great care must be taken in choosing heaters or combined heater/thermostats. They must be of the right wattage in relation to the volume of water. In my experience, most hobbyists choose a unit that is too powerful. The heater must be capable of raising a given volume of water to the required temperature, and keeping it at this level.

Discus fish need a temperature of 29 to 30°C. If it falls below this level, the fish will show certain kinds of discomfort, like poor colour and poor feeding, and may even develop some ailments. (*Spironeucleus* is often associated with too low a temperature).

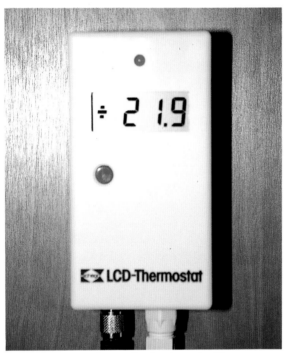

Schego external electronic thermostat.

Heater/thermostats of too-high a wattage have often caused the death of the fish. In bi-metal type of control units, the elements gradually wear out, and as a result the thermostat 'sticks'.

This means that the heating element is operating continuously and if the heat loss from the aquarium is not equal to the heat produced by the element, the temperature of the water inevitably rises. With a wattage that is too high, the water can easily be raised to more than 38° to 40°C, which is bound to be fatal to Discus fish.

It is generally accepted nowadays that 0.5 watt will maintain the temperature of one litre of water in a warm room, and that 1 watt per litre will be sufficient in a cold room. As a safety precaution, many experienced Discus keepers also connect a pre-set heater/thermostat to an electronic thermostat which is set a few degrees higher. If the bi-metal control units fail and the heater/thermostat ceased to switch off, the electronic thermostat will cut in. Although such a duplicated system may at first sight appear unnecessarily extravagant, it has, to my knowledge, saved many hobbyists from disaster. The cost of such a unit will never be more than the replacement cost of just one or two adult Discus fish; and if it prevents the loss of a whole aquarium of fish, then it certainly cannot be considered too expensive.

It is also advisable to use two heater/thermostats of smaller wattage in one aquarium, rather than one high-wattage unit, as it is very unlikely that both units will fail at the same time. I have also found that a blob of silicone sealant at the bottom part of the heating element will stop the heater from breaking, especially in a clinical set-up, when the suction cups are no longer sticking well to the sides of the glass.

I have also found that many heater/thermostats fail to operate normally as soon as colder weather sets in; and many hobbyists, instead of waiting for something to fail, replace all heating units as a matter of routine at this time.

LIGHTING

In recent years, many new types of aquarium lights have become available. Apart from fluorescent tubes, hobbyists are now also offered mercury vapour lamps and metal halide lamps in different shapes and sizes. Mercury vapour and metal halide lamps are not really needed for the basic Discus aquarium we have been considering; they are really more suited to a large, well planted-up aquarium. The Discus fish themselves are not greatly concerned about the amount of light they receive: on the whole they seem to prefer a fairly subdued light. Discus, in fact, always look their best when there is very little overhead light; but especially when natural daylight, falling on to the tank, catches their bodies. The use of a too-powerful light source will always result in the fish losing their strong coloration.

If there is to be no plant life in the Discus fish aquarium, fluorescent tubes should be the first choice. They can easily be installed in the aquarium cover or suspended 10 to 15 cm above the aquarium. In our 130 x 60 x 60 cm aquarium, two 40-watt fluorescent tubes should be adequate. These tubes are also available in many different sizes, from 30 cm to 200 cm, and in many different colours; the actual choice of colour will depend on the individual but the tubes most frequently used are either 'Truelite', claimed to be the closest possible match to daylight, or 'Growlux' which will somewhat intensify the red coloration. Other colours which are normally also stocked by fish shops are 'Northlight', a somewhat bluish light, 'Warmwhite' with a yellowing effect, and 'Daylight', also somewhat more yellow than 'Truelite'.

Although these fluorescent tubes seem to last for a very long time, they will have lost 50 % of their output within the first six months or so, and therefore should be frequently replaced.

If, however, the Discus fish are to be kept in a furnished aquarium containing live plants, fluorescent tubes may not be powerful enough to provide the plants with the energy they need. Fluorescent tubes are really only suitable for planted aquariums with a water depth of not more than 45 cm. In taller tanks, the light will not be strong enough to penetrate far, resulting in poor plant growth. In shallow tanks, two or three 'Truelite' fluorescent tubes may provide adequate intensity of light for the plants to flourish, but in taller tanks, a different light source must be provided.

Depending on the actual depth of water, the choice should be between mercury vapour lamps and metal halide lamps. The new miniature metal halide spots are often ideal for purposes of display. These light fittings should be suspended from the ceiling or wall, 30 to 40 cm above the aquarium. The spread of light very much depends on how they are installed, and the hobbyist should consult a competent electrician.

Mercury vapour or metal halide lamps have on average a life of about 5000 hours, after which they will need changing. Although they also produce a certain amount of heat this should not affect the aquarium in any way.

When using mercury vapour or metal halide lamps, one should acclimatize the live plants slowly to this type of light. If one were to copy nature and provide the aquarium with 12 hours of light, right from the start, most of the plants would very quickly die. As most aquarium shops keep their plants in either trays or badly lid tanks, the shock of suddenly been given such an intensity of light seems to prevent the plants from getting established. It is therefore advisable to provide only five hours of light per day, for the first week or so. During the second week, the light can be left on for another hour; during the third week, for two more hours, and during the fourth week, for a further two more hours. In my experience, 10 hours of lighting per day, using this type of light source, is usually enough to maintain aquarium plants in good conditions.

Final adjustments may be necessary after several weeks, when one can easily tell whether the plants are doing well, from their colour, and from the presence of photosynthesis; this is shown by small oxygen bubbles rising from the leaves, an indication that the chlorophyll in the plants is converting carbon dioxide and water into carbohydrates and oxygen under the influence of light. Very seldom can photosynthesis be observed when fluorescent light fittings are being used: it is good evidence that the light source is adequate.

Growing plants must, of course, also be provided with nutrients otherwise they will very quickly exhaust themselves; it is pointless, however, even though it is common practice, to fertilize aquarium plants when they are no longer doing well. If aquarium plants do not flourish, a fertilizer will seldom make them grow better. There is something amiss, but it is seldom a lack of nutrients.

ULTRA-VIOLET RADIATION

Ultra-violet sterilizers have been used in aquarium keeping for some considerable time. They destroy many types of bacteria, though they are not able to keep the aquarium germ-free. They are especially useful in the preparation of 'breeding' water, and are generally only used for this purpose. Since ultra-violet radiation that is too powerful and prolonged can damage eggs and embryos, it must be used with great care in the breeding aquarium. The use of an ultra-violet sterilizer can, however, also be recommended for clearing a newly set up aquarium of any cloudiness due to bacterial or algal bloom.

Ultra-violet radiation units are available in different sizes, and are either air-operated or linked to the return pipe of a power filter. Their working life is between 5000 and 7500 hours of continuous operation; then the tube has to be replaced.

OZONE

Ozone is a very powerful oxidizing agent, capable of freeing the aquarium not only of bacterial or algal bloom, but also of certain diseases. However, it is often very haphazardly used: hobbyists are rarely able to assess accurately enough how much ozone should be used; consequently either very little oxidation takes place, or too much ozone is produced. An excess amount of ozone gas released into an enclosed space is very dangerous to humans, and can be responsible for afflictions ranging from strong headaches to serious illness.

Ozone can be produced by means of a machine called an ozonizer. Used at its right level, it is more effective than ultra-violet radiation. It speeds up the oxidation process so much that the interim products in the nitrification cycle, such as nitrite, are not produced at all. It will oxidize not only any dead organic matter polluting the water, but also many essential trace elements and vitamins, and even the mucous on the fish. Therefore ozone should not be used in a breeding tank with either eggs, or with very young fish.

THE OXYDATOR

This new device appeared on the market

several years ago and was both hailed as a very useful addition to fishkeeping, and condemned as a useless piece of equipment. As there are always several opinions about anything, especially in fishkeeping, it is not surprising that the technical experts could not reach a unanimous verdict.

The oxydators used for aquarium come in two sizes, a small size for 100 litres of water, and a larger size for up to 400 litres of water. The inner plexiglass container of the oxydator is filled with a 3% or a 6%

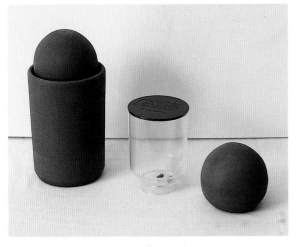

solution of hydrogen peroxide. It also contains one or two clay pellets and has a small hole in the base. When filled, the container is sealed, and then put upside-down in the outer ceramic vessel. The whole device is then immersed in the aquarium.

The clay pellets contain manganese dioxide, which catalytically changes a very small amount of the hydrogen peroxide into pure oxygen and water. The resulting pressure forces small quantities of the hydrogen peroxide solution through the small hole into the ceramic vessel.

When this solution comes into contact with the vessel, the manganese dioxide present in the ceramic converts it into oxygen and water, providing a continuous supply of pure oxygen to the aquarium water. An oxygen bubble keeps the solution from escaping from the oxydator, and aquarium water from entering, and makes the device absolutely safe for aquarium use.

Hydrogen peroxide is inexpensive and easy to obtain. One filling of it should last for several weeks, depending on the temperature of the water, and its degree of pollution. An oxydator should prove a useful addition to any aquarium, for increasing the oxygen content of the water and thereby making the biological filtration more effective. It should also prevent the build-up of anaerobic bacteria which otherwise would soon make the closed system of the aquarium break down. As the well-being of the Discus fish is highly dependent on biologically sound and healthy water, the use of an oxydator must be recommended.

An oxygen-measuring test will clearly show the amount of oxygen dissolved in the water at any one time, and should be frequently used as a check.

FILTRATION

No subject causes more argument in fishkeeping than filtration. I do not know whether this is because some hobbyists are unable to keep up with modern trends, or because they are just not willing to change their methods because 'things have always worked that way'.

There are those who assert that the best outside power filter is the only one that should be used; others contend that some keepers or even breeders do well without using any filtration at all. They usually fail to add that those keepers or breeders change a great deal of the water every day; a change of 90% of the water twice a day seems normal practice in some of the Far Eastern countries, where not only is the water of a more generally suitable quality, but there is also a cheap labour force to carry out this task.

It may even be that hobbyists are sometimes misled by so-called 'technical writers' or 'experts' who themselves do not understand the subject; there is no other way of explaining an assertion made some time ago by a writer in one of the English fishkeeping magazines, to the effect that charcoal was no better than filtering wool, but was always recommended by the shop assistant because the profit margin was higher.

It hardly matters what the quality of aquarium water is to start with: it soon becomes burdened with fish urine and waste, food and other decaying matter, and filtration must be used. I myself have very strong views regarding the type and combination of filters most suitable for Discus fish, but it is for each hobbyist to make his own choice; the only criteria must be efficiency and reliability.

UNDERGRAVEL OR SUBGRAVEL FILTERS

These are operated either by an air-pump, or a power filter head. The filter is placed on the bottom of the aquarium and covered with a layer of gravel: the recommended thickness of the gravel is usually 5 cm. The water passes through the gravel which retains any particles of uneaten food or waste, and returns to the aquarium via the up-lift tube. A build-up of aerobic bacteria in the top few millimetres of the substrate converts all the accumulated waste into harmless substances.

This, at any rate, is the theory; but in practice it all looks quite different. Since the water follows a path through the gravel bed where there is least resistance, usually only a very small area of the whole substrate is used. The larger part, with hardly any oxygen-rich water passing through it, becomes a breeding-ground for anaerobic bacteria. The subgravel filter also needs to consume a large amount of oxygen used by the bacteria for their function of nitrification: this amount of oxygen is not usually available, and so the organic substances in the gravel bed are not oxidized. The substrate becomes 'blocked up' and the number of anaerobic bacteria increases considerably. Many of their metabolic products are very toxic; and with hydrogen sulphide, methane and other substances in the filter bed, the system will break down completely and the substrate becomes black with a putrid smell.

Although the subgravel filter can be 'run in' quicker than any other system, it will also invariably be exhausted sooner than any other. Then the aquarium will have to be completely emptied out; the gravel will have to be either discarded and replaced, or thoroughly washed and set up again. The fish, however, having become acclimatized to the slow deterioration of the water quality, will always suffer greatly from 'fresh-water shock'.

In spite of their many disadvantages, subgravel filters are still commonly used; their only real advantage compared to any other system is that they are very inexpensive and not visible in use. But they should not be used in any installation containing Discus fish.

AIR-OPERATED INTERNAL FILTERS

The box types of air-operated internal filters are either square, triangular or round and the water passes through the container using the 'airlift' principle. They can be used as mechanical, chemical or biological filters, and can be filled with charcoal, peat, filtering wool or any biological substrate. When the filtering material is soiled or exhausted, it can quickly be renewed. However, because of their small size, and the small amount of filtering material they can hold, they are not really suitable for a Discus fish aquarium, except perhaps for a small hospital tank.

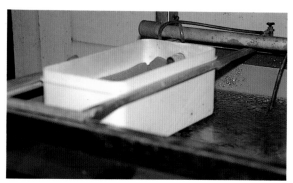

The 'only' filtration used in one of Thailand's Discus fish farms.

A sponge type of air-operated internal filter is often used by Discus fish keepers. These sponges come in various sizes and with a suitable air-pump can even be used in quite large installations. They provide mechanical and biological filtration, and the large surface area of these sponges allows large numbers of bacteria to get established. All types of sponge filters need very little maintenance. Once every two or three weeks the sponge cartridges must be removed and rinsed out under lukewarm water: cold or very hot water will destroy the useful bacteria within the sponges and must not be used. These sponge type filters are often used in hospital tanks or as supplementary filters in breeding tanks. Their efficiency can be greatly increased by the use of an oxydator.

POWER-OPERATED INTERNAL FILTERS

There are many different types available to the hobbyist, although they all work in the same manner: water is sucked through a filtering cartridge contained within a filter box. The filters are operated by a centrifugal pump-head, which in some filters allows variable amounts of the water to pass through. They are attached to the inside of the aquarium by means of suction cups, in such a way that the cleaned water is returned to the aquarium at the surface level, creating a gentle movement.

In some filters, the intake openings can be closed, either to reduce the turnover, or to prevent dirty water from running back into the aquarium when the filter is removed. The filtering cartridge is not difficult to replace, and can be used several times, after thorough cleaning. The Eheim internal power filter also offers additional filter modules and cartridges, which can extend the unit to practically any size.

The only disadvantage of these filters is that they can only be used with the sponge cartridge supplied, and not with any other kind of filtering material. The advantages that they have over any air-operated filters are their neat design, ease of maintenance and totally silent operation.

Although such units are used in many Discus fish set-ups, and especially in smaller breeding tanks, I feel that they are usually not efficient enough to obtain the purity of water that is needed; they should only be used where a 'polisher' is sometimes needed.

EXTERNAL POWER FILTERS

Again, there are many different types available to the hobbyist, but they all work on the same principle. The aquarium water is continuously circulated through the filter container, which is filled with mechanical, chemical or biological filtering material or any combination of these. Dirt particles and suspended matter, as well as dissolved pollutants, are retained by the filtering materials, and only clean water is

returned to the aquarium.

The modern types of centrifugal pumps have very few moving parts, a high output with a very low current consumption, and a silent operation. The only maintenance required is the cleaning of the impeller under running water, once in a while.

In the past, great importance was always attached to the turnover of such power filters. Today, I think, many more hobbyists are aware that the size of the actual filter container and the contact time with the filtering material are more important. In many Discus fish installations, a dual or even triple system is used; several filtering container are linked up in sequence. The larger volume of filtering materials used ensures a much longer operation, with greater efficiency. With the hose connectors, shut-off taps, etc., that are available, a reasonably neat installation can be achieved. These multi-container systems are always run with only one power unit; and a further advantage is that the containers can be changed or cleaned one at the time, leaving the bacteria colonies undisturbed in the other ones.

The size of the power filter should be determined by the volume of water in the aquarium. The full amount of water ought to pass through the filter one or one-and-a-half times per hour. A smaller turnover will produce the needed purification, whereas a larger turnover often creates too much turbulence.

The choice of any power filter for a Discus aquarium must be made with the following considerations in mind: the filter must completely fulfil its task of purifying the water, and it must be absolutely reliable. From personal experience over many years, I have found that some makes are more reliable than others, and the hobbyist should consult a competent retailer about this. It is pointless to buy a power filter which, soon breaks down, and, though it may still be under warranty, takes several weeks to be repaired. The hobbyist can only really afford to buy equipment which will be exchanged, and not just repaired, if it breaks down while still under warranty. And finally, the choice must depend on the greatest availability of accessories. Only a power filter that meets all these requirements is really suitable for a Discus fish installation.

TRICKLE FILTERS

Trickle filters have suddenly become the 'in thing', even though they have been used in large-scale water treatment for a long time. Their sudden popularity can only be due to the recent work carried out by Dupla of West Germany: the only two models of trickle filters that are commercially available are manufactured in West Germany by AB Aquatechnik and by Dupla Aquaristik.

Although trickle filters are more commonly used in seawater installations, they are also very useful in Discus fish tanks. I first used a trickle filter with Discus fish more than 15 years ago; compared to today's complex designs, it was a rather simple affair. It consisted of a channel running the whole length of the aquarium, in which cleaned water from a power filter was trickled, by means of a spray-bar, on to a biological filtering material. The water would be collected

Internal trickle filter.

on one side of the aquarium, and flowed back via a fine filter.

Today's trickle filters are more sophisticated. The commercially available models may not be suitable for one's particular installation; most hobbyists either have them manufactured to their specification, or actually build them themselves. These filters are generally installed either underneath or above the aquarium, or inside the aquarium.

A trickle filter is by far the most effective biological filtering system available today. In full operation — and it takes three to four weeks for a colony of aerobic bacteria to be formed — it will convert almost all the dissolved metabolic substances into nitrogen, without depleting the water of its oxygen content, as would happen in a closed system. In fact, the water returning to the aquarium is enriched with oxygen, due to the availability of atmospheric oxygen, which is able to enter the filter. The very toxic ammonia is converted by the bacteria into relatively harmless nitrate.

The aerobic bacteria continue to multiply, being constantly supplied with dissolved metabolic substances from the passing aquarium water. Depending on the pH value of the water, some species of bacteria reproduce themselves within minutes, while others take several hours. The pH value of the water should never fall below 6.5 when using a trickle filter since bacterial purification at a lower level would no longer take place.

One of the most important factors affecting the efficiency of a trickle filter is the flow rate of the water. This must be great enough to prevent the filter from drying out, but not so strong that the settled bacteria are washed away from the filtering media. Dead bacteria, however, are washed from the substrate, and collect as sediment.

SYSTEM FILTERS

By system filters, I mean an installation where several aquariums or banks of aquariums are maintained by one filtering system. Such a system usually contains a mechanical unit, a biological unit and a unit that carries out water purification through ion exchange, as well as an ultra-violet radiation unit. It can also be connected to a mains water supply and a drain, in such a way that a small but continuous amount of fresh water is constantly supplied to the system.

Such a system is quite easily put together from various plastic pipes and fittings obtainable from builders' merchants. The aquariums can either be run on the overflow principle, or in new installations holes can be drilled into the glass at suitable places. All the water from the aquarium is made to flow into a ring-main and then into the filter proper. From there it is pumped up again, using a submersible rotary pump. The pump must be connected to a float switch, to prevent it from running dry. Also, the filtering container must be large enough to take all the excess amount of water from the tanks in case of pump failure. By means of stopcocks on both the outlet and the inlet pipes, each tank can be isolated from the system, in case of disease, or for maintenance purposes.

Such a system is expensive and is only worth installing if at least six tanks are to be linked together. But in such case, since the water quality in every tank must be identical, the fish can be moved from tank to tank without causing them any stress whatsoever.

FILTERING MATERIALS

The various filtering materials perform different functions. Not only do they remove dirt particles suspended in the water; they also remove dissolved substances like protein, nitrite, nitrate, medications, etc., and also colorants by adsorption. There are some materials which perform a purely biological function as well as enriching the water with essential substances. I shall deal with the main filtering materials in sequence.

MECHANICAL FILTERS

Mechanical filtering materials are used either as a coarse pre-filter or as a fine post-filter. Pre-filter materials are usually nylon netting, which retains the dirt particles suspended in the water; it

does not, however, retain any of the substances dissolved in the water. Another type of mechanical filtering material often used is a hollow ceramic material, which looks rather like cut-up macaroni. The water passing through this material will be deviating from the direction of the main current and will therefore hold back any coarse dirt particles.

The amount of mechanical materials used as a coarse pre-filter in any filtering system should be 25% of the total volume. It can be reused after rinsing in water for a considerable time. The effectiveness and durability of the main filtering material greatly depends on the presence of a mechanical pre-filter.

The fine post-filtering material is usually a synthetic wadding: glass or cotton wool must not be used. The fine filtering material retains even the smallest dirt particles. Its efficiency greatly depends on the degree of pollution of the aquarium water.

The fine filter wadding cannot be thoroughly cleaned, and so must not be reused; it should be changed frequently. When medications are applied to the aquarium, only properly cleaned coarse pre-filter and new post-filter materials should be used.

CHEMICAL FILTERS

Chemical filtering materials, like charcoal and ion exchange resins, work by adsorption. They remove from the aquarium water many of the dissolved substances, like protein, nitrite, nitrate and even ammonia; and they prevent the water from becoming turbid as a result of overfeeding, with a consequent unpleasant smell. They also, of course, remove any of the applied tonics, trace elements, vitamins, peat extracts and other beneficial additives.

Any carbon type of filtering material will in time also take on the function of a biological filtering medium, though it can never be as effective as a specific biological filtering material. Carbon must, moreover, be frequently changed. Exhausted carbon material can release the absorbed substances, partially decomposed, back into the aquarium as toxins.

Carbon material must first be soaked in hot water, to expel any air trapped within it, and then rinsed several times in cold water to free it from any dust. The active life of the filter very much depends on the quality of the material, and it must be changed when the water no longer looks 'white' but has a yellow tint.

Carbon filtering material are not really suitable for Discus fish installation as they often raise the pH value of the water to the neutral point; they could be used, perhaps, once in a while, for a day or so, to 'polish' the water. But carbon is always used after treating the aquarium with any medication; it cannot be used again, and must be discarded.

Another type of chemical filtering material which is often used advantageously with Discus, is peat. This not only enriches the aquarium water with essential humic and organic acids and hormones, but also lowers the hardness and the pH of the water. But only peats specially prepared for aquarium use are really safe. Many of the ordinary garden peats may contain traces of fertilizers or weedkillers which would have disastrous consequences for Discus fish.

Aquarium peats are usually available in a mild or a stronger form. Their suitability can be checked by soaking some peat in water overnight. If the pH value of the water does not show a substantial drop, the peat is not suitable for aquarium use. About one litre of peat should be allowed per 100 litres of water. The pH value and hardness of the water must be checked regularly and the amount and type of peat used changed accordingly.

When peat is used as the main filtering material in a power filter, a suitable pre-filter as well as a fine post-filtering material must be used. The peat must be changed every four weeks, or when there is no longer any difference between the pH values of the main aquarium water and the water that has just passed through the filtering material.

ION EXCHANGE RESINS

There are certain types of ion exchange resins that are able to remove ammonium and nitrate from the water. However, they must be carefully chosen. Some are not suitable to soft water; others have proved to be harmful to Discus fish. With ion exchange resin something is exchan-

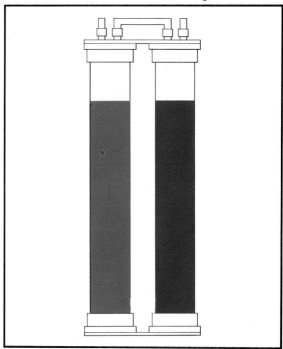

Two-column deioniser; the only really satisfactory way to produce a consistently large quantity of suitable water.

ged for something else: in the case of a nitrate exchanger, for example, nitrate is exchanged for the regenerant, sodium chloride (common salt), and some toxic substances are leached back into the water shortly before complete exhaustion.

The resins most often used for this purpose are manufactured in West

Germany by Bayer Chemicals. Two types are available: Lewatit M 600 which also removes the humic acids from the water and Lewatit MP 600, which does not.

One litre of either of these resins is able to remove 30 g of nitrate from the water, and should be used in 100 litres of aquarium water. It must be regenerated, every three months or so, by using 300 g of cooking salt dissolved in three litres of warm water (about 30° to 40°C). The regenerant is trickled through the resin over a period of about one hour, and then the resin is washed with four to five litres of mains water, again over a period of 1 hour.

Ion exchange resins are used as the main filtering material in power filters, but must be protected by a good pre-filter, and a fine post-filtering material must also be used. The resins have proved to be successful, but they should be used only by experience aquarists.

BIOLOGICAL FILTERS

Biological media are any materials in which a colony of aerobic bacteria can form and carry out the function of purifying the water. For any aquarium, this is the most efficient type of filtration and should be used in every Discus fish installation.

The materials must have good adhesive properties, to encourage the bacteria to settle; they will then multiply into large colonies ensuring a quick decomposition of all dissolved harmful substances, into relatively harmless matter. Biological purification of the water needs, however, large amounts of oxygen. If biological purification takes place in an enclosed system (power filter), the oxygen content of the water must be relatively high, and the installation of an oxydator is recommended. If the biological purification of the water is achieved by using a trickle filter, the bacteria will take the required oxygen

Hair-rollers a biological filtering material.

from the atmosphere, without diminishing the oxygen content of the water to any great extent.

Almost anything can be used as a biological filtering material, so long as it offers a good adhesive surface to the bacteria. Suitable for aquarium use are: coarse rough gravel; lava, or any other inert porous material; phenol-free sponge; Dupla's Bioballs; ICI's Flocor RS Biomedia — or even ladies' plastic hair-rollers!

In an enclosed system, the biological materials must be protected by a coarse pre-filter and also by a fine post-filtering material. The bacteria colony will be established within a few weeks, and the filter should be left running until an appreciable reduction of turnover is noticed: in a single-unit system, this will be in about four to six weeks. The filter must then be cleaned. The pre-filter material is thoroughly washed; the biological material is rinsed under luke-warm water, and the fine post-filtering material is renewed. In a multi-container system, with the pre-filter regularly serviced every month or so, the biological material will remain effective for 6 to 10 months.

In an open trickle filter system, with the pre-filter cleaned at regular intervals, the main biological material is almost self-cleaning and requires no attention.

The choice of biological materials must to some extent depend on what is available. For the Discus fish installation, the ideal is a maintenance-free biological substrate; and if at all possible, a trickle filter should be used.

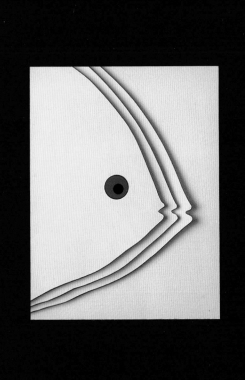

WATER CHEMISTRY

GENERAL OR PERMANENT HARDNESS ●
CARBONATE OR TEMPORARY HARDNESS ●
THE pH VALUE

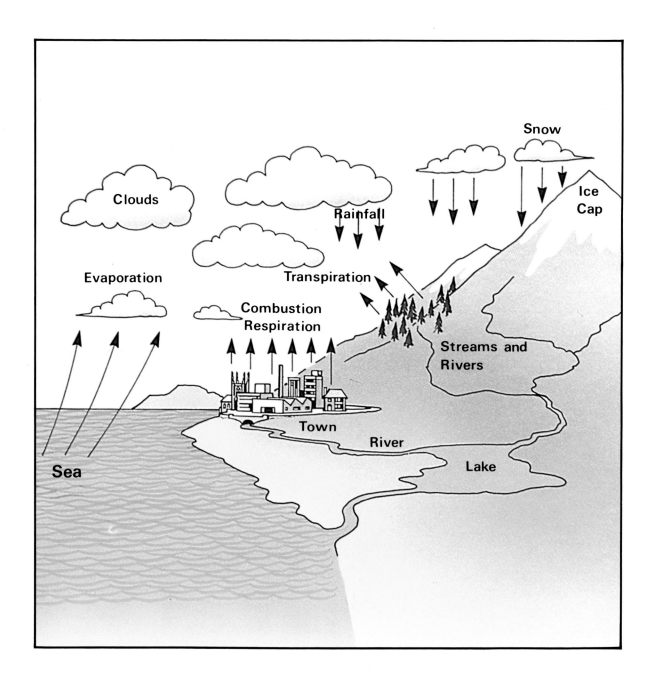

It is important for the aquarist to have some understanding of the nature and composition of water.

In its pure form, water (H_2O) is an oxide of hydrogen : $2H_2$ (g) + O2 (g) → $2H_2O$ (1). As it contains no traces of dissolved salts, it does not conduct electricity. This pure water is also totally 'dead', and cannot support life.

Drinking water whether from the mains or from other sources, however, is never pure, in the chemical sense; it always contains small amounts of gases like oxygen and carbon dioxide, as well as some dissolved solids which give the water a degree of hardness.

Water moves in a never-ending cycle around the earth, in the oceans, rivers, lakes and the air. It evaporates into the atmosphere and forms clouds, which are condensed water vapour; eventually it is precipitated as rain, snow or sleet. As these precipitations return to earth, they adsorb not only oxygen and carbon dioxide, but also many other gases from industrial pollution. As the water comes into contact with the various layers of the soil, it is enriched with many biological substances from, for example, peat or humus; and also with cations like calcium and magnesium, as well as anions like sulphates, carbonates of hydrogen and others. These cations and anions give the water its hardness or electrical conductivity.

GENERAL OR PERMANENT HARDNESS

The general or permanent hardness of the water is due to the total concentration of calcium (C + +) and magnesium (Mg + +) ions. These are the two dominant cations affecting the hardness of the water. If the water contains only small amounts of these cations, it is termed 'soft'; if it contains large amounts, then it is termed 'hard'.

Although other cations, such as sodium and potassium, may be present,

they do not increase the hardness of the water and their overall effect is negligible.

In Europe the hardness of the water is usually expressed in dH. One degree of dH represents 10 mg of calcium oxide (CaO) or magnesium oxide (MgO) dissolved in one litre of water. In the USA, the water hardness is expressed in ppm (parts per million) of total dissolved solids, and is equivalent to 1 mg of calcium carbonate ($CaCO_3$) dissolved in one litre of water.

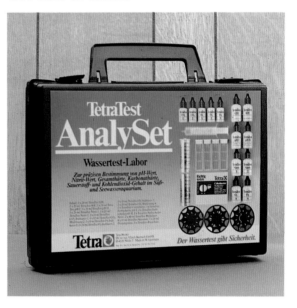

Water is graded according to its dH value as follows:

up to 3 dH __ soft
3 – 6 dH __ medium soft
6 – 10 dH __ slightly hard
10 – 16 dH __ medium hard
16 – 26 dH __ hard
over 26 dH __ very hard

To test the water for general or permanent hardness, either a conductivity meter or a drop test is used. With a conductivity meter, all dissolved salts are measured, and are expressed in microSiemens/cm at 25°C. One microSiemens/cm corresponds to the conductivity of a solution of approximately 0.5 mg of sodium chloride (NaCl) or 0.1 mg of hydrogen chloride (HCl) per litre of water. A general comparison between conductivity and dH can never be very accurate, but for fishkeeping purposes, 35 microSiemens can be taken to equal approximately one degree of hardness.

To test the general hardness or permanent hardness of the water with a drop test, a specific amount of water is used in a measuring vessel. The reagent solution is added, drop by drop. The first few drops will turn the water red; the test is completed when the red changes to green. The total number of drops used is the total amount of general or permanent hardness expressed in dH, one drop being equal to one degree of dH. For a more accurate measurement, the amount of testing water can be doubled, with one drop representing only one-half-degree of hardness.

CARBONATE OR TEMPORARY HARDNESS

The carbonate or temporary hardness of water is due to the hydrogen carbonate (HCO_3) ions in the water, which may come from three sources: the reaction of free carbon dioxide with water; the reaction of mineral carbonates with free carbon dioxide and water; and as the product of bacterial reduction processes.

Carbonate or temporary hardness can easily be removed from the water, either by boiling it, when the bicarbonates will decompose to form insoluble carbonates commonly called 'fur' or by filtration through peat.

It is most important that the water used in Discus fish installations should have a sufficient degree of carbonate hardness. The buffering effect of this type of hardness keeps the water at a stable pH value. In heavily burdened water with little or no carbonate hardness, the pH value can drop to a dangerously low level, becoming acid enough to kill the fish.

To test for carbonate or temporary hardness, a specific amount of water is used in a measuring vessel. The reagent solution is added drop by drop until the water turns first blue, then yellow. The

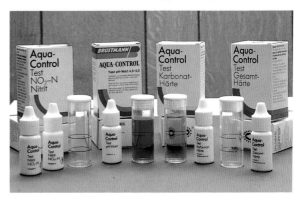

total amount of drops used represent the total amount of carbonate or temporary hardness of the water, one drop being equal to one degree of carbonate hardness. For a more accurate measurement, the amount of testing water can be doubled, with one drop only representing one-half-degree of hardness.

Aquarists often suppose that when a total hardness value is given, this represents the carbonate hardness of the water, together with the sulphate level. This is not the case: 'total hardness' means the Ca + + and Mg + + cations only, just as 'carbonate hardness' means only the hydrogen carbonate (HCO_3) anions.

However, it is possible for the carbonate content of the water to be higher than the non-carbonate content, so that the HCO_3 anions more than balance the Ca + + cations; in which case, the hardness of the water represents the HCO_3 excess only.

In most cases the raw water available to the Discus fish enthusiast is too hard and must be adjusted. If the anion content of the raw water is high, the hobbyist could soften it by filtering through peat, or by boiling. However, if large quantities of water are needed, these methods are not practicable.

The simplest way to soften water is by the addition of prepared rainwater or of demineralized water. If raw water with 10 dH hardness is mixed with an equal amount of demineralized water, the resulting water will have only 5 dH of hardness. Thus by adding mineral-free water to raw water, the hobbyist can achieve any degree of hardness that he needs.

In the very rare cases when water has to be made harder, this can be achieved by adding to it small pieces of unpolished marble chippings, dolomite stones, or some specific aquarium additive such as Dupla's Hardness Bildners, one tablet of which will raise the general and/or carbonate hardness of 50 litres of water by one degree.

THE pH-VALUE

The pH value of the water is the measure of the quantities of hydrogen ions effectively present in it. The pH scale ranges from 0 to 14. In water with a pH below 7 (the neutral point), more acid substances are found than in a water with a pH value above 7, where more alkaline substances are found. In neutral water, the acid and base substances cancel one another out. The pH scale is logarithmic (tenfold), so a drop in the pH level from the neutral point to pH 6, means that the water has become ten times more acidic.

Therefore, any changes in the pH value of the Discus aquarium water must be carried out with great care. Most Discus fish should be able to tolerate a slight change of the pH value of the water, as long as this is gradual; any sudden drop will result in clouding of the eyes, burning of the fins and loss of the mucous membrane of the fish. No Discus fish should ever be kept in water with a pH lower than 5 or much higher than 7.5. The Discus fish keeper and breeder should aim for a pH value of between 6 to 6.8.

In many Discus fish installations, a drop in the pH value occurs as a result of biological degradation of the water, and the lack of bicarbonates. The bicarbonates act as buffers, binding all the acids in the water, and giving a more stable pH level. It is therefore most important that any very soft water used for Discus should contain some bicarbonates, to prevent the water from becoming too acidic.

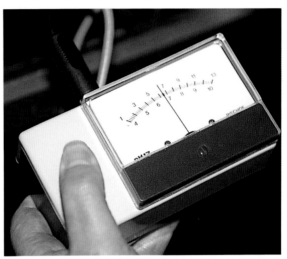

Electrical pH meter for more precise measuring, giving an instant read-out.

The hobbyist has several means of effectively lowering the pH value of the water. He can use one of the commercially available pH adjusters; but some of them will also increase the hardness of the water and should be avoided. Or the water can be filtered, using peat. The addition of either hydrochloric or phosphoric acid will also reduce the pH level, and so will the water from the cation exchange resin column of a two-column deionizer. I have always used the last method, and have found that very small quantities were needed.

If the pH level of the water is too low, it can be raised by strong aeration to expel all the carbon dioxide (CO_2), or by the addition of lime stone or sodium bicarbonate. One can also buy pH adjusters which can raise the pH level to any desired degree.

In the case of a Discus fish aquarium, the adjustment of the pH level up or down must be done very gradually and with

This Schmidt-Focke bred Red Turquoise breeding pair was the first to be imported into England by Mr. E. Schulze.

great care, and constantly monitored by means of a pH-testing kit.

To test the pH value of the water either an electrical meter, test paper or a drop test can be used. The modern electrical meters often have a digital display, which gives an instant read-out when the electrode of the meter is dipped in the water. Electrodes are subject to ageing, and have a life of two years at most, after which they must be replaced. The tip of the electrode must always be kept submerged either in distilled water or in a solution of potassium chloride (KCl) to prevent it from drying out. The use of a electrical pH meter will give the hobbyist the most accurate readings.

When test paper is used, a strip is dipped in the water and compared with a colour chart. Several types of these test papers are available. Some only show whether the water is acid or alkaline; other kinds display the whole range of values from 0 to 14. The best one to use would be test papers showing values from pH 5 to pH 7.5. Test papers can only be used once.

To test the pH value using a drop test. A specific amount of water is placed in a measuring vessel. A specific quantity of test solution, of which there are several makes, is added to the water drop by drop. When the colour of the water has changed, it can be compared with a colour chart. Very acidic water is usually red, while very alkaline water is usually dark-green to blue.

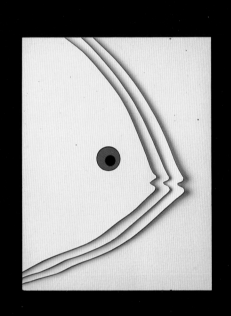

WATER

RAINWATER • AQUARIUM PEAT • WATER
SOFTENING OR DEMINERALIZATION WITH
ION EXCHANGE RESINS • WATER
SOFTENING UNITS • TWO-COLUMN
DEIONIZER • REVERSE OSMOSIS

Amazonas.

To have any real long-term success with keeping or breeding Discus fish, the hobbyists should know something about water and water chemistry. In the natural habitat of the Discus, the water has a pH value varying from 5.5 to 6.8, and very low conductivity. This water is therefore almost like commercially available deionized water, or rain water. It is known, however, that Discus fish are generally quite adaptable, and there should be no need to provide them with an exact copy of their natural water. Experience suggests that they will remain healthy and even propagate in a water with a somewhat higher degree of hardness.

This does not mean, however, that Discus can be kept in whatever water comes from the mains, since this varies greatly from area to area. Even in the Greater London area, water can be found with a hardness as low as 11 dH and as high as 23 dH. The pH values of these waters will also range from the neutral point (pH 7) to pH 8.6. In other parts of Great Britain, the water may vary from very soft — 2 dH — to very hard — over 30 dH. My own London mains water has a carbonate hardness of 14 dH, a total hardness of 23 dH, and a average conductivity of 650 μS, and a average pH value of 7.6 (during the course of the year the pH can vary between 7.2 to 8.1). The same variations can be found in many countries on the Continent of Europe and in the United States. In Germany, for instance, the softest water may have only one-third-degree of hardness, while the hardest water may have a dH of almost 40.

In the Far East, the water is usually rather softer than in Europe; it does vary from place to place, but without these great extremes. The water used by one of the most successful Discus breeders in Bangkok, Thailand, has a carbonate hardness of less than 1 dH, a total hardness of 3 to 4 dH, a conductivity of 100 to 130 μS and a pH value of 7. Except

for a slight adjustment to the pH, this water is used straight from the tap. However, a few miles away, at the other side of Bangkok, another Discus breeder has to provide his fish with deionized water, because his mains water has a carbonate hardness of 4 dH, a total hardness of 9 dH and a pH value of 8.1.

People often ask me whether Discus fish can be kept in mains water, without telling me what the composition of the mains water is in their part of the country. By now it should be quite obvious that mains water in the greater part of Great Britain is highly unlikely to be suitable, and that an alternative supply should be arranged.

RAINWATER

It is often said that rainwater is ideal for Discus fish keeping, but I have never found this to be the case. Rainwater usually contains too many toxins which would prove fatal to the Discus. Even if one could rely on being able to collect enough rainwater to give the fish the necessary water changes, a great deal of time and effort would have to be spent on making this water safe.

Rainwater is usually collected from the roof of an outhouse or in a specially rigged-up rainwater tank, where a great deal of dust and other matter will also have collected over a period of time. This dust, etc., must be removed before the water can be used for the fish. Even then, the collected rainwater must first be filtered with a specific ion exchange resin or carbon, to free it from all the dissolved harmful substances deriving from industrial pollution. Also, rainwater is 'dead' water, and needs the addition of organic substances like humic acids, colloids and chelates to mature it biologically and make it safe for Discus fish.

The effort involved in the preparation of rainwater and its often unreliable supply, make it a bad choice for a Discus fish installation, where a great deal of water is needed.

AQUARIUM PEAT

One method of softening water for Discus fish is by the use of peat, which can be used either in a stocking in a reservoir tank, or as the main filtering medium in a power filter. Peat will not only remove the carbonate hardness, but will also acidify the water. Any water can be softened by means of a suitable peat, but the large quantities sometimes needed would turn the water such a strong brown colour that it would be almost impossible to see into the aquarium.

Consequently, peat is a good filtering material for Discus aquariums, but can only be recommended for softening water when just a slight adjustment of the water quality is necessary. In water with relatively high hardness and pH level, the use of peat as the chief softening medium is unlikely to be successful.

WATER SOFTENING OR DEMINERALISATION WITH ION EXCHANGE RESINS

The use of ion exchange resins in the preparation of water goes back a long way. This method of bringing water to a particular condition needed for fish-keeping is now considered by many to be preferable to all other procedures.

Ion exchange resins are used in the form of solid, insoluble granules or beads. They adsorb ions from a solution, and at the same time desorb an equivalent amount of other ions. However, the exchange of ions can only take place between ions of a similar charge. Cation exchange resins will only exchange cations, and anion exchange resins will only exchange anions. This takes place as the water (or any other solution) passes through the resin bed. As all ion exchange resins have a limited capacity, they must be regenerated when

exhausted so that they can be used again.

Ion exchange resins fall into two groups: cation exchange resins and anion exchange resins. These groups can be further divided into strongly acidic or weakly acidic cation exchangers and strongly alkaline or weakly alkaline anion exchangers. The different types of resins have different total capacities, and react differently to pollutants and organic matter. Not every ion exchange resin is suitable for the preparation of water for fishkeeping and only 'established' resins should be used for this purpose. Two types of ion exchange resin units are available to hobbyists: the disposable type, or the type that can be regenerated.

The disposable type of unit always contains both the cation exchange resin and the anion exchange resin in a proportion, depending on the capacities of the resins, such as to give mineral-free water with a pH value just below neutral. The low pH is the result of some leakage of mineral acids as well as carbon dioxide in the water (which can be expelled with aeration or heat). As disposable units are often filled with inferior resins or even 'reject' resins, care must be taken when using the water: it must always be tested for the hardness and pH values before use. Unsuitable deionized water can be more harmful to the fish than unsuitable raw water.

The capacity of disposable units is often very low; although they are quite inexpensive, in prolonged use the replacement cost makes them uneconomical.

WATER SOFTENING UNITS

When a water-softening unit is used, the ion exchange resin exchanges any hardness-causing ions like calcium and magnesium ions, for a 'soft' ion, usually sodium. After being exchanged for the equivalent proportion of sodium ions, the calcium and magnesium ions are retained in the resin. Because of the sodium carbonates, sulphates and bicarbonates that are now present in the water, its pH value will be higher than that of the raw water; but though it can be called 'soft' the total mineral content has not been changed.

Water from a softening unit where the resins are supplied in the sodium form, is not suitable for fishkeeping. The prepared water is always much worse than the raw water and is only fit for use in conjunction with detergent, as in washing machines and dishwashers.

If the ion exchange resin is supplied in the hydrogen form, all the calcium and magnesium ions are exchanged for an equivalent proportion of hydrogen ions. Although the water will show a reduction in the total mineral content, the pH value will usually also be very low, due to the formation of many mineral acids and carbon dioxide. In most cases, a great deal of raw water will have to be used to bring the pH value to a tolerable level; this will again increase the total hardness of the water to such a degree, that all one's trouble will have been for nothing.

All of the commercially-available water softening units, and even the ion exchange resins are of no use at all to the serious Discus fish keeper or breeder. The only really satisfactory way to produce a consistently large quantity of suitable water is with a two-column ion exchange unit.

TWO-COLUMN DEIONIZER

The advantage that a two-column deionizing unit has over a mixed bed unit (in which cation and anion resins are mixed) is that it can be regenerated by the hobbyist in situ. The often very involved exchange procedure for the mixed-bed unit can make it only the second choice.

In a two-column deionizer, the cation exchange resin and the anion exchange resin are kept separately and regenerated separately; the ease of operation makes such a unit the first choice for any hobbyist needing large quantities of water for the maintenance of Discus fish.

In its operation, the two-column deionizing unit is connected with a length of tubing to a raw-water supply. The water passes through the cation exchange resin, and all mineral salts in the water are exchanged for an equivalent amount of acids. This mineral-free water then enters the second column, filled with the anion exchange resin, where almost all the acids are exchanged for hydrogen, oxygen and carbon dioxide, giving a pure water with a slightly acidic value, due to the presence of carbon dioxide, and to a slight leakage of mineral acids from the anion resin bed.

The first column is filled with a strongly acidic cation exchange resin. The ion exchange resin most often used for this purpose is manufactured in West Germany by Bayer Chemicals. Their Lewatit S100 G1 colour-indicating cation exchange resin has a polystyrene matrix crosslinked with divinyl benzene, and carries sulphonic acid groups. It has a high operating capacity, giving perfectly conditioned water even at low level regeneration. The advantage of this cation exchange resin, compared to many others is that it shows that it is exhausted by unmistakably changing colour; there is therefore no need for expensive testing equipment to monitor the quality of the water.

This cation exchange resin removes all the mineral salts from the raw water and exchanges them for their equivalent acids. Approximately two litres of resin gives about 6000 to 7000 BV of completely demineralized water. (BV = Bed Volume, i.e. litres). On exhaustion, the colour of the resin changes from golden to red.

To regenerate two litres of exhausted cation resin, about 10 litres of a 6 to 10% solution of hydrochloric acid is needed. After the resin bed has been backwashed (by reversing the flow of water) for several minutes, to free it from air and other matter, the regenerant solution is passed through it for about 30 minutes. The colour of the resin then returns to its original gold. Next, the regenerant solution is rinsed out with about 20 litres of raw water during approximately 30 minutes, or until the red colour shows in the first few centimetres of the resin bed.

This cation exchange resin is reasonably stable, and can be regenerated again and again. Like most other exchange resins, it must not be allowed to dry out, and should be kept from freezing.

The column can be made of perspex or glass. Before filling it with resin, one should make sure that there is already some water in the column; and also, that the resin still contains some moisture, because dried-out resin is apt to fracture on contact with water, and so become unfit for further use. As some types of resin expand on exhaustion or on regeneration, a gap must be allowed above the resin bed; this gap is also needed when backwashing the resin before regeneration.

During backwashing, the resin flows freely in the upward stream of the water, until all air pockets and other debris have been removed. After backwashing, the resin bed should be allowed to settle, after making sure that it is completely covered with water; otherwise channelling may occur in use, producing incomplete contact between the water and resin. The output of deionized water will then be reduced.

If the unit has not been used for some time, all the water contained in it, as well as the first few litres of processed water, should be discarded. The ideal flow rate of Lewatit S100 G1 is 40 BV per hour. In a two-litre resin column 80 litres of water should be passed through. The flow rate can be increased by up to 50% with very little change in either the quantity or the quality of the water.

The second column of the two-column deionizing unit is filled with an anion exchange resin. The resin most often used is Lewatit MP 62, manufactured in West Germany by Bayer Chemicals; it is a weakly basic, monofunctional anion exchange resin. It has outstanding thermal, mechanical and chemical stability, with a constant high operating capacity even at low-level regeneration. The resin has a macroporous structure and its polystyrene matrix enables it to adsorb organic substances and desorb them completely during regeneration.

To equal the capacity of two litres of cation exchange resin, three litres of anion exchange resin are needed, resulting in a mineral-free water, with a pH level of just below neutral. This low pH level is due to some leakage of mineral acids, as well as to carbon dioxide which can be expelled from the water with aeration or heat.

The pH level of the water may fluctuate to some extent during the operating cycle, being neutral or even slightly alkaline at the beginning, and becoming more acidic towards the end. If the water is being collected in a reservoir tank, the small variation of the pH will not matter, since the overall pH will remain always in the slightly acidic range.

To regenerate three litres of exhausted Lewatit MP 62 anion exchange resin, 10 litres of a 3 to 5% solution of sodium hydroxide are needed. After the resin bed has been backwashed for several minutes with water from the cation exchange column, to free it from all trapped air and other matter, the regenerant solution is passed through for about 30 minutes. Next, the resin bed is rinsed for 25 to 30 minutes with 30 litres of water from the cation exchange column.

This anion exchange resin is very stable, and has a high capacity and a comparatively low carbon dioxide content. It must, however, only be regenerated or rinsed out with completely demineralized water, or water which has first passed through the cation exchange resin.

I myself prefer the Duolite A303 anion exchange resin, which can be regenerated and rinsed with raw water without greatly affecting the performance of the resin, or its capacity.

Duolite A303 is a weakly based anion exchange resin, and is mainly used in conventional two-column exchange units. It has mixed tertiary amino and quaternary ammonia groups. It has a very high regenerating efficiency, but needs to be rinsed with a very large volume of raw water; or with a smaller amount of fully demineralized water, or water from the cation exchange column.

The combination of Lewatit S100 G1 cation exchange resin and Duolite A303 anion exchange resin in a two-column system has proved in my experience over many years capable of supplying completely demineralized water of a quality suitable for Discus fish keeping, and in sufficient quantity.

Deionized or demineralized water is dead water, and must never be used on its own in Discus fish keeping, but must always be blended with a certain amount of raw water, to increase the hardness of the water to a suitable level. Before use, it must also be aerated vigorously to expel the carbon dioxide; the pH level will then rise almost to the neutral point. If large quantities of deionized or demineralized water are combined with a little raw water to maintain a degree of hardness, it is also advisable to add a generous amount of water conditioner, humic acids and trace elements, to make the water biologically more sound.

It is often claimed that Discus fish kept in deionized or demineralized water do not display the same coloration as fish kept in more natural water. In fact, Discus fish kept in well-prepared deionized or demineralized water are as colourful and as willing to spawn and raise their young as fish in natural water. By using a two-column demineralizing unit many hobbyists should for the first time be able to maintain, breed and rear Discus fish where before they had failed.

REVERSE OSMOSIS

Although the principle of water purification by reverse osmosis (RO) is quite recent, compared to the use of ion exchange resins, there are already units available for the aquarium hobby. Unfortunately, these units have a very low capacity, and are therefore not practicable. The first unit I ever used, specially developed in the USA for aquarium use, produced only about one litre of water in 24 hours. The advantage, however, is that any desired hardness of water can be produced by a simple adjustment.

In reverse osmosis, the water passes through a membrane. The membrane material used for water purification are cellulose acetate, cellulose triacetate and polyamide, and are either spiral wound or hollow fibre. Of the raw water that passes through the membrane, the greater part is waste water (90 to 95%) and the rest is RO-treated water; it still has a small mineral content, with an average pH of about 6. The RO units needs backwashing every 24 hours, and can, in principle, be used continuously for ever.

However, since most of the models at present available are for commercial use only, and the only model for aquarium use has an inadequate output, the use of reverse osmosis for Discus fish keeping cannot, as yet, be recommended.

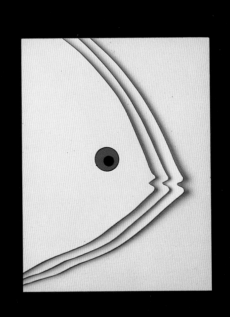

THE NITROGEN CYCLE IN THE AQUARIUM

AMMONIFICATION ● NITRITE ● NITRATE ●
OXYGEN ● IRON

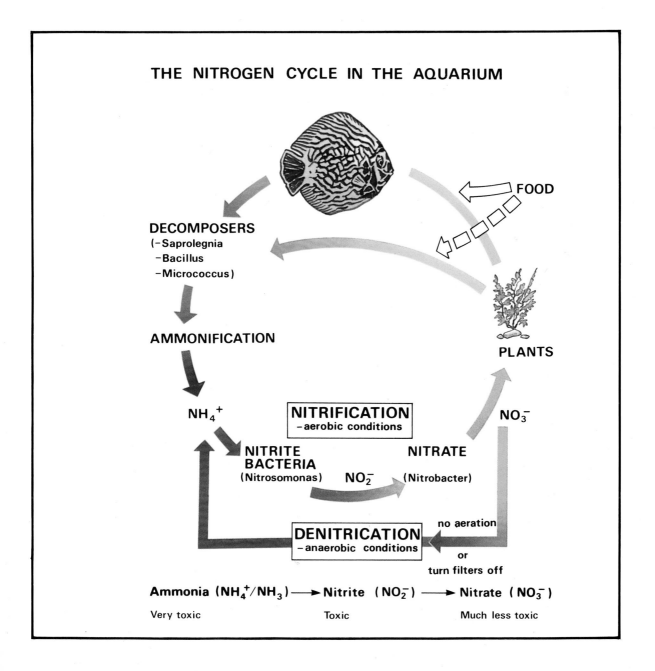

THE NITROGEN CYCLE IN THE AQUARIUM

FOOD

DECOMPOSERS
(-Saprolegnia
-Bacillus
-Micrococcus)

AMMONIFICATION

PLANTS

NH_4^+

NITRIFICATION
-aerobic conditions

NO_3^-

NITRITE
BACTERIA
(Nitrosomonas) NO_2^- (Nitrobacter)

NITRATE

no aeration

DENITRICATION
-anaerobic conditions

or
turn filters off

Ammonia (NH_4^+/NH_3) ⟶ Nitrite (NO_2^-) ⟶ Nitrate (NO_3^-)

Very toxic   Toxic   Much less toxic

Bacterial activity in the aquarium has already been mentioned several times in connection with filtration and filtering materials; but for a fuller understanding of the function of nitrite, nitrate and ammonia in the aquarium, it is necessary to look at the nitrogen cycle in greater detail.

Because of uneaten food, fish waste and rotting plants, the aquarium water come to be burdened by many harmful substances, a build-up of which could be fatal to the fish. But the presence of certain bacteria in the water or substrate gives it 'self-cleaning' power to neutralize these harmful substances. These bacteria belong to two main groups: heterotrophic and autotrophic.

The heterotrophic bacteria convert organic substances into ammonia (NH_3) and ammonium (NH_4), this is the first stage of biological purification. In the second stage, the autotrophic bacteria, *Nitrosomonas*, oxidize the ammonia to nitrite (NO_2); the *Nitrobacter* oxidize the nitrite to nitrate (NO_3). The third stage of the nitrogen cycle is the process of denitrification, when, as a result of shortage of oxygen, anaerobic bacteria take over from the aerobic bacteria, and by biological reduction, convert the relatively harmless nitrate to the very toxic nitrite and nitrogen (N_2).

As bacteria are present everywhere, in the air, in the water and in the substrate, a relatively quick build-up can be achieved. In a completely new installation, I have always found that the use of an oxydator and the addition of small quantities of flake food for several days help to establish a good colony of bacteria. In this way, when the fish are introduced, after a week or so, the usual initial high build-up of nitrite can largely be avoided. It normally takes at least three to four weeks for the nitrifying bacteria to be established in such numbers that the process of purification becomes biologically stable; in oxygen-rich water, the process is greatly speeded up. Daily measuring of the nitrite and nitrate content of the water will give the hobbyist the best indication of when it will be safe to introduce the fish into the aquarium.

Any new aquarium must be given a running-in period, so that the biological processes can get established. A speeding-up of the initial 'running-in' period can be achieved through 'grafting'; this means the use of some substrate from an established aquarium, or of a small amount of biological filtering material from a old filtering system. As the substrate or filtering material will already have been colonized by bacteria, this hastens the process of making the aquarium water safe.

Once the biological processes have been established, they must not be disturbed. A good amount of oxygen dissolved in the water makes the biological purification more effective. If biological filtration should stop working for any length of time, it will be starved of oxygen-rich water, and the aerobic bacteria contained in the filter will die. Anaerobic bacteria will form, and will convert nitrate to nitrite, and then to ammonia. If the filter should again start working — for instance after a power cut lasting several hours — the aquarium would become totally polluted with toxic substances.

It is therefore important to remember that when a filtration system has been stopped for several hours, the biological material must be properly cleaned, and the coarse pre-filter and fine post-filter ing materials must be renewed.

The addition of certain types of medicines to the aquarium water will also destroy the nitrifying aerobic bacteria, bringing about a rapid build-up of a high nitrite content; so daily checks must be carried out.

AMMONIFICATION

In the first stage of the nitrogen cycle,

the highly toxic ammonia is changed to the non-toxic ammonium. The toxicity, however, depend greatly on the pH level of the water. As all Discus aquarium water should have a pH level of neutral or below, there should be no possibility of ammonia poisoning.

Ammonia and ammonium can be tested for with a commercially available tester. A certain quantity of reagent powder is mixed with a given amount of water; after a while the water will change colour. By checking this colour change against a colour chart, the amount of ammonia and ammonium present in the water can be determined. Ammonia and ammonium can be removed by changing water, and by more efficient biological filtration.

NITRITE

In the second stage of the nitrogen cycle, the toxic nitrite is oxidized by bacteria into the relatively harmless nitrate. Although Discus fish can tolerate a high nitrite level for a short time, the aim should be to provide them with nitrite -free water.

Nitrite can be tested for with a commercially available tester, which works in much the same way as the ammonia tester just described; except, instead of using a reagent powder, two separate reagent solutions are used.

A high nitrite content may be the result of overstocking, of overfeeding, or of a breakdown of the biological filtration system. Nitrite can be removed by changing the water, or by treatment with ozone and with certain types of activated carbon.

NITRATE

Nitrate is the harmless end-product of the nitrogen cycle. It is much used by plants as a fertilizer, but in a plant-free aquarium, it will often cause a build-up of algae. Nitrate can be tested for with a

commercially available tester, which works in the same way already described for ammonia and nitrite testing.

Nitrate can be removed by changing the water, by the use of nitrate-removing resins, and by growing plants.

The information given by nitrate readings about the quality of Discus aquarium water can be summarized as follows:

below 20 mg nitrate — clean and healthy water
20 to 40 mg nitrate — water is still acceptable
40 to 80 mg nitrate — partial change needed
80 to 150 mg nitrate — 50% water change needed
over 150 mg nitrate — the water is heavily burdened and dangerous for fish, because of denitrification

In many parts of the world the nitrate content of raw water is very high, and there the Discus fish keeper is well advised to check even the water which is going to be mixed with prepared rain water or demineralized water. It has sometimes been found, that the addition even of small quantities of raw water could be harmful to the fish. In such cases, the use of a nitrate-removing resin in preparing the water would be absolutely necessary.

OXYGEN

Oxygen is a colourless, odourless gaseous element. It makes up approximately 21% of the atmosphere, but is only slightly soluble in water. Water at a temperature of 30°C contains only about two-thirds as much dissolved oxygen as water at 10°C. In an aquarium the oxygen content of the water is all-important; as well as keeping alive the fish and other aquatic life, it is the most important factor in the purification of water, giving rise to a healthy aquatic life-cycle. If the oxygen content of the water should drop to a very low level, the fish will eventually die of suffocation.

Low levels of oxygen concentration are usually caused by pollution; therefore organic and inorganic waste must not be allowed to collect. The biological filtration system, which uses the greatest part of the dissolved oxygen, must never be allowed to become an oxygen trap, but should be carefully maintained.

Low oxygen levels in a Discus fish aquarium can be recognized when the fish are gulping for air at the surface of the water. An excess of carbon dioxide in the water has a similar effect, which can often be observed after a large, careless water change. In Discus installations, the aim must always be a 70 to 80% oxygen saturation: to increase the oxygen level, the hobbyist can install a more powerful aerator, a power filter with a spray-bar, a trickle filter or an oxydator.

Oxygen concentration in water can be measured with an electrical meter; this has a special electrode which is dipped into the water, and a read-out which displays the result. As such meters are still rather expensive, the hobbyist will usually resort to a drop test. An oxygen drop test has four different reagents; it needs skillful handling, and takes about 30 minutes. Although the results can never be as accurate as that obtained with an electrical device, they are sufficient for the purpose; the test should be carried out at least once a week. The result not only shows the percentage of oxygen dissolved in the water but gives timely warning of danger.

IRON

Many trace elements are needed to sustain life in a Discus aquarium, especially if the water is soft to begin with; but iron plays a particularly important role. It gives aquatic plants their lush, green coloration; moreover,

experiments conducted in Germany by Dr. E. Schmidt-Focke and others have shown that if Discus fish are kept in water containing dissolved iron, the red coloration is greatly improved.

Iron is found in all natural waters but most aquariums have a shortage of it. In a Discus aquarium, it should be present in a concentration of 0.5 to 1.0 mg per litre. I have kept Discus fish in water where the iron content was much higher (2.5 mg/l), but the extra iron did not seem to cause any additional improvement in their coloration. Iron in a well-planted aquarium is quickly consumed by the plants, and is also precipitated through oxydation, so the iron content of the water should be topped up, daily or weekly.

A drop test for iron content is available: a reagent solution is added, drop by drop, to a measured amount of water, and the resulting colour change is checked against a colour chart.

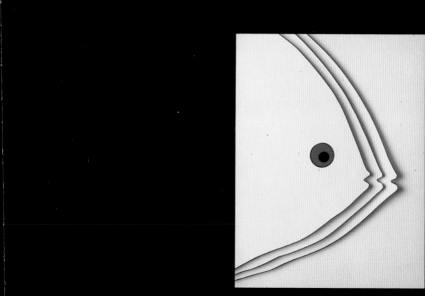

DISCUS FISH IN A FURNISHED AQUARIUM

DECORATIONS

Most newcomers to Discus fish keeping like to install their charges in a furnished aquarium of some kind, rather than keep them in a clinical environment. Even if they are already aware that such an installation may create many problems, especially at the beginning, they can never be persuaded to start with an aquarium without any furnishings at all.

A completely unfurnished aquarium is always easier to handle. The amount of food that the fish need can be monitored so precisely that within a very short time one knows exactly how much to give. One can also see much more clearly how the fish waste gradually accumulates, because it does not get lost in the gravel. Any adjustments to the quality of the water are also less of a problem, since no other factors are involved.

However, as most beginners cannot or will not see the advantages, they should, at least, learn how to go about furnishing an aquarium.

The use of decoration like 'sunken galleon', 'treasure chests' or 'spinning water-wheels' depends on individual taste: what is important, however, is that anything used in Discus fish water should be chemically inert, or beneficial, like bogwood. Decoration of a more appropriate kind include: nicely shaped 'safe' rocks without any sharp edges; slate, again with the sharp edges filed away; cork bark, which, because of its buoyancy, must be securely anchored to the aquarium or held in position with heavy rocks; and bamboo canes, fixed to a drilled base-plate, with both ends sealed with either a resinous varnish or a blob of silicone sealant to prevent rotting.

What is probably more commonly used in furnished Discus aquariums than any other kind of decoration is bogwood, which is available in many sizes, colours and shapes. The twisted root-like pieces make a very effective and often convincing copy of an Amazonian biotope. I have seen many splendid Discus fish aquariums which contained only this type of decoration. Hobbyists, as a rule, do not just go out and buy a number of pieces; they spend much time rummaging through heaps of bogwood in the shop in order to find just the right pieces.

Bogwood can be found in a variety of colours, from the rather light type to an almost black variety. The lighter-coloured bogwood usually comes from either the Irish or Scottish peat bogs and is more solid in form. The very dark brown to black variety with its many tangles originates in Europe, but is not always easy to find, especially in Britain. Another variety, also very dark brown and often with twisted roots, sold everywhere in Britain as Amazonian bogwood, comes in fact, from the Far East, where it is collected in the mangrove swamps.

All decoration used in an aquarium must be safe for the fish. Rocks and slate must be inert, that is, they should not leach out any minerals, and especially, hardness formers into the water. To make sure of this, immerse them in hydrochloric acid — there should be no reaction. Any sharp edges or corners must be filed or sanded away, so that the fish would not injure themselves, should they

Nine-weeks old German-bred Turquoise Hi-fin Discus.

bump into the rocks in a fright, or should they rub themselves against them due to some minor body ailment or irritation. Before being introduced into the aquarium, the rocks and pieces of slate should be scrubbed with a hard brush and thoroughly hosed down, to remove dirt and any loose particles.

Cork bark and bamboo canes need no other preparation than a cleaning with water and a brush to remove any dust or soil.

Bogwood, whether from peat bogs or mangrove swamps, should be dead wood. After any loose particles have been scraped off with a hard brush or even a knife, they must be soaked in water until they sink: usually this is all the preparation that is needed. Some types of bogwood may release a great amount of humic acids and other organic substances as well as dye, and must be soaked for a considerable time, sometimes as long as several weeks. The water should be changed several times, and the bog-

wood should not be put into the aquarium until the soaking water stays fairly clean and clear. If the bogwood is introduced into the aquarium too early, not only can they release acids which become a hazard to the fish; but the dye tints the water so strongly that the fish will be difficult to be seen.

The lighter-coloured Irish or Scottish type of bogwood often contains parts which are not dead, showing up as almost white patches. These patches must be removed; the simplest way to do this is to drill them out with a small electric hand-drill. If they are left, they invariably become mouldy and although this will not be fatal to the Discus fish, it will certainly have an effect on the quality of the water. Hobbyists using this kind of bogwood in their aquariums, will sometimes give it several coats of a polyester type of varnish; once this is completely dry, the bogwood can be introduced into the aquarium and is usually safe for a very long time.

PLANTS FOR THE DISCUS FISH AQUARIUM

*APONOGETON ● BARCLAYA ●
CERATOPTERIS ● CRINUM ●
CRYPTOCORYNES ● ECHINODORUS ●
HYGROPHILIA DIFFORMIS ● MICROSORIUM
PTEROPUS ● NYMPHAEA STELLATA ●
SAGITTARIA*

Of the many kinds of aquarium plants that are to be found, only a few are suitable for the Discus fish aquarium. Even if we adjust the water somewhat away from the condition ideal for the fish, to a degree of hardness of about 8 to 10 and a pH value of between 6 to 7, only a limited number of aquatic plants can be used, because of the high water temperature needed by the fish. Bulk selections of plants sometimes offered to the Discus fish hobbyist by nurseries, often include varieties which will not tolerate these water conditions.

When an aquarium is to contain both Discus fish and plants, a choice has to be made at the outset whether the well-being of the fish or the cultivation of the aquarium plants is to be more important. No Discus fish aquarium can ever look like some of the beautifully stocked underwater 'gardens' one sometimes sees; but with careful selection, one can achieve a compromise where the plants will complement the Discus fish, and give a pleasing picture. The one point to remember, though, in this kind of installation, is that the planted aquarium must receive a more intense light, and must also be fertilized with iron or carbon dioxide or both, for sustained growth.

The following aquarium plants are the varieties usually recommended with the proviso that the water must have a hardness of 10 dH, with a pH value of 6 to 7 and a temperature of around 29°C.

APONOGETON

APONOGETON. Most of these plants are suitable for the Discus fish aquarium, especially *A. crispus* and *A. undulatus*; they grow well in the water quality and temperature that the Discus need. All *Aponogetons* have a corm, and will grow for six months or so, when they will have to have a rest period of several months, kept in the dark in damp peat. They can then be replanted and will quickly grow their new leaves. They are also the aquarium plant most ready to flower. *Aponogetons* at this temperature will need additional fertilizing with iron, otherwise the large leaves will suffer from chlorosis and will quickly die away. *A. ulvaceus*, however, is not suitable, as it will not tolerate the temperature.

BARCLAYA

BARCLAYA *longifolia* is a good contrast plant and is the only red variety of plant which is suitable for the aquarium. With its long, slightly ruffled leaves, it looks most effective in front of a thicket of green *Echinodorus*. At this water quality and temperature it often does not develop to its proper size, but stays somewhat smaller; however, it is still a good plant for the Discus fish aquarium.

CERATOPTERIS

CERATOPTERIS *thalictroides*, the Indian Fern, can be either used as a floating plant or planted in the substrate. As a floating plant, it will soon spread out; planted, it often looks thin and spindly. It makes very few demands as to water quality and temperature. When used in breeding tanks with baby Discus fish it helps to maintain low nitrate levels.

CRINUM

CRINUM. Also known as Onion plants: of the 160 or so known species, two types are usually available, *C. thaianum* and *C. natans*. *C. thaianum* with its long straight green leaves is one of the most undemanding plants for the Discus fish aquarium. It will grow to more than 200 cm and must be cut back from time to time. Care must be taken when planting, not to put the bulbous roots too deeply into the substrate, otherwise they will rot away and the plants will die. *C. natans*, the African Onion plant, with its ruffled dark green leaves, has never really done well in Discus aquarium water: it seems to thrive only in much harder and cooler water.

Crinum thaianum, the Thai Onion plant will grow to more than 200 cm.

CRYPTOCORYNES

CRYPTOCORYNES. Most *Cryptocorynes*, with their different size leaf shapes and colours, make ideal plants for the aquarium. Some are very easy to grow and make no special demands, others have to be handled more carefully and given special attention. Some do better if used as potted plants, rather than as a loose plant; *C. cordata*, for example. They must all be slightly shaded if they are to stand upright, and the addition of iron in the water will produce good specimens, often with many runners.

C. affinis has shiny dark green lanceolate leaves, brown to reddish on the underside. It is a fast grower and undemanding, producing many new shoots. It grows to about 12 to 15 cm, and therefore should be used as a medium-sized foreground plant.

C. aponogetifolia has long, narrow, crinkled, light green leaves. It is a slow grower; the mature plants are suitable for background only, with the leaves lying on the surface of the water. It grows to more than 60 cm in height and 5 cm in width. Regular iron and carbon dioxide fertilization will maintain its beautiful green coloration.

C. beckettii has short brownish leaves, reddish on the underside. A reasonably fast growing plant, it will in time form dense clusters. It grows to about 10 to 15 cm.

C. blassii has oval shaped brown to reddish leaves on a long stem; the underside is purple-red. It grows to about 25 to 30 cm. Only potted plants are recommended for use at this aquarium temperature.

C. ciliata has long light green leaves on a long stem. In good light, it is an easy and reasonably fast-growing plant. It grows to 45 to 50 cm, and should be used for the background only.

C. griffithii has dark green to brown egg-shaped leaves, sometimes spotted, on a stem. It is often very difficult, and only potted plants are recommended; it grows to about 10 cm.

C. parva has small, pure green lanceolate leaves on a very short stem. It is a slow grower, but once established, the plants will form many runners; if planted too closely, it may collect to much mulm. It grows to only 2 to 3 cm, and is a lovely foreground plant.

C. petchii has dark olive-green to brown short-stemmed leaves; a relatively fast growing plant with many runners,

Echinodorus bleheri, the Large Amazon Sword, undemanding, but needs feeding in a Discus fish aquarium.

Most Cryptocorynes, with their many leaf shapes and colours are most attractive.

Hygrophilia difformis, water Wisteria, will not only 'sweeten' a new installation but also remove nitrate from the water.

Cryptocoryne aponogetifolia, a slow growing plant but will grow to more than 60 cm.

which normally grows to 15 to 20 cm in height, but in a Discus tank, never to much more than 10 cm.

C. wendtii has olive-green to brown lanceolate leaves with wavy edges. It is relatively easy to grow, reaching only about 5 to 7 cm in height: a foreground plant.

C. willisii has green lanceolate leaves. It is easily grown, and will stay small, only about 4 to 5 cm, and so is a foreground plant.

ECHINODORUS

ECHINODORUS. This is also called the Amazon Sword plant. Many of its different varieties are suitable for a Discus fish installation. Some grow very tall and are used as solitary plants, while others stay very small and are used as a carpet-like foreground covering. All Amazon Sword plants are very heavy feeders, and the addition of iron to the water at regular intervals is the only way to maintain their growth; otherwise, the new leaves will always be stunted and transparent.

E. amazonicus has light green, narrow, lanceolate leaves, and is probably the easiest to grow of all the Amazon Sword plants. It is a very bushy plant; imported plants often have more than 12 to 15 leaves. Two or three plants can be grouped together. It will grow to about 25 to 30 cm.

E. bleheri dark green, with broad, lanceolate leaves; with iron regularly added to the water, it is fairly undemanding, but in the aquarium will grow only to 35 to 40 cm. It should produce many new leaves, but if they are stunted, it is a clear sign of iron deficiency, or of a too-high temperature.

E. quadricostatus, with its short-stemmed, narrow lanceolate leaves will grow to about 10 to 15 cm. It is relatively easy to grow; two or three plants grouped together give a good effect.

E. rubra. This still rather rare Amazon Sword plant, with its big leaves, is very variale. Sometimes imported plants will not take at all; at other times, they settle down very easily. It should always be a background or solitary plant, and seems to do better with iron crystals or Duplarit K in its substrate.

E. tennellus is the real dwarf amongst the Amazon Sword plants. It has narrow light green leaves, and will, with good lighting and feeding, send out many runners, and forms a very short carpet-like covering. For its continuous growth, it must have plenty of nutrients.

Although *Cryptocorynes* and *Echinodorus* will between them supply enough variety to the aquarium, there are a few other plants which should be included. All will grow well without needing any special attention.

HYGROPHILIA DIFFORMIS

HYGROPHILIA difformis, Water Wisteria, is probably one of the most suitable plants for the Discus fish aquarium. It will grow well planted, or can even be used as a floating plant, to provide some darker areas in the tank. Three or four stems bunched together make an attractive display and will often very quickly reach the top of the aquarium. To stop the plants from growing any further, the crown must be pinched off. Water Wisteria is propagated from cuttings. When it is used as a floating plant, care must be taken that no food is trapped between the leaves.

I have always used this plant in Discus fish aquariums to 'sweeten' the water at the start; and also in breeding tanks, to reduce the build-up of nitrate or to eliminate slight clouding of the water. Water Wisteria is such a useful aquarium plant, that no Discus fish aquarium should be without it.

MICROSORIUM PTEROPUS

MICROSORIUM PTEROPUS, Java Fern, is a very undemanding plant which puts up with the temperature and the water quality of a Discus aquarium. It is a reasonably fast-growing plant and will do well even in a subdued light. A few plants anchored to the bogwood or rocks with rubber bands will give a nice effect, with their short-stemmed lanceolate dark green leaves, speckled with black markings. The plant propagates itself by producing offsets along the edges of the leaves as well as on the root system. As it takes its nutrients almost completely from the water, a fertilizer must be added regularly.

NYMPHAEA STELLATA

NYMPHAEA STELLATA, with its reddish leaves, also looks well in the aquarium. This plant has a tendency to grow floating leaves, but if they are cut off early enough, a bushy effect can be achieved.

Nymphaea stellata has a tendency to grow floating leaves.

The corm of *N. stellata* needs a rest period after about six months or so, and should be removed from the aquarium and kept moist. However, even when the corm has almost completely dried out, it seems to recover again and again. It is a nice decorative contrast plant in the aquarium; but also a heavy feeder.

If a narrow-leafed plant is wanted, any of the varieties of *Sagittaria* should be suitable. *S. platyphila*, *S. pusilla* and *S. sabulata* will grow well in the temperature and hardness of Discus aquarium water. These plants are, however, very buoyant and must be securely anchored to the substrate until the roots have grown long enough to keep them in position. All *Sagittaria* are fairly heavy feeders, and the addition of iron to the water will maintain their beautiful green coloration. Once the plants are established, they will send out many runners.

All the plants listed have been successfully grown in Discus aquarium water of various degrees of temperature, hardness and pH values, and have lived sometimes for as long as five years, with minimal maintenance.

Obviously, sometimes one type of plant does not take, but this is rarely due to the conditions in the installation, but rather to the particular plant. It may have been damaged during transit, it may have been kept out of water for too long; or it may have been just a bad plant.

Sometimes other types of plants are offered for Discus fish installations; for instance, *Cabomba*, *Anubias* and various types of *Vallisneria*. I have found, over the years, that none of them is really suitable. They often survive for a short time, but then die away completely.

There may, of course, be many other plants able to thrive in a Discus fish aquarium, but this is something the hobbyist must find out for himself.

A suitable plant must be able not just to survive for a little while, but to show actual signs of growth and be able to propagate itself.

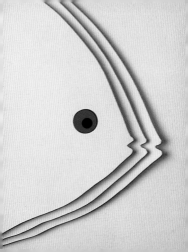

PROBLEMS WITH ALGAE

BROWN ALGAE ● *GREEN ALGAE* ● *BLUE - GREEN ALGAE*

Some Discus fish keepers have aquaria which are constantly afflicted with algae; whereas there are others who have never encountered algae at all. Algae are the result of many different factors and can be kept under control by applying a regular maintenance routine.

Algae are primitive living plants. If the more complex plants in the aquarium are flourishing, because the condition of the water, the lighting and the number of plants stocked are all exactly right, there exists a state of biological balance, and algae should not cause any problems.

Even in such a well-balanced installation, pinhead-sized spots of algae may form on the rocks and on the sides of the aquarium. These are nothing to worry about, and so long as they do not seem to be constantly increasing, no action is necessary. They can be removed by gently scraping.

Real algae problems do, however, occur in many new installations until a biological balance has been achieved in the aquarium.

BROWN ALGAE are probably the easiest to control: they occur only when there is not enough light, and may rapidly cover the sides of the aquarium, the leaves of the plants, and the rocks or bogwood.

The algae can be scraped with a special scraper from the sides of the aquarium and wiped from the leaves with a sponge or with the fingers. They can be prevented from forming again by increasing the lighting: not only in duration but possibly also in intensity. A new installation needs about 10 to 13 hours of light at the right intensity, out of every 24 hours. The light can usually be reduced

by one or two hours after the first months, or once the plants have become established in the aquarium. If brown algae continues to form, a second or even third light source may be necessary.

Brown algae will often form in a clinical Discus fish set-up where there is no plant life at all, or just one or two plants in flower pots: this is due to the lack of a proper balance. In such cases, the addition of a liquid peat extract will usually prevent brown algae from forming again.

GREEN ALGAE are always the result of too strong a light. By simply reducing the lighting in duration by one or two hours, or in intensity, this problem can usually be eliminated. The addition of fast-growing plants like Water Wisteria will also reduce the algae, if a very fine adjustment is all that the biological balance needs.

BLUE-GREEN ALGAE are also found in Discus fish aquariums, and are always the result of bad maintenance and over-feeding. Blue-green algae will only form when the aquarium water contains a high nitrate level; especially when there is a high phosphate level. Frequent water changes, less food, more efficient filtration and fast growing plants will rid the aquarium of this type of algae.

To control algae, there are several chemical treatments available to the hobbyist, but their use in a Discus fish aquarium should not be necessary, since most algae problems can easily be resolved by the installation of a time-switch, the use of peat extracts, frequent water changes and a more efficient filtration system.

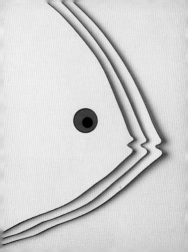

OTHER SUITABLE FISH

There are several species of fish which would make suitable companions for Discus fish in a display aquarium, and many other species which would not do at all: so the choice should be made only after careful considerations.

Some fish are fast swimmers and eaters, and by the time the Discus fish start to feed, most of the food will have been eaten. Other fish are easily intimidated by Discus and will probably hide. Some kinds of fish, like Angel fish, should under no circumstances be kept with Discus fish; not only because of their aggressive nature, but also because of the diseases that they often give the Discus.

If other fish are introduced, they need not be of the Amazonian varieties, but they must be able to stand the higher temperature, the hardness and pH value of the water. But the paramount consideration in planning a mixed furnished aquarium must always be to ensure that the Discus fish are the focus of the collection.

I have seen many mixed aquariums which not only brought Discus fish into contact with a great number of other kinds of fish, but contained certain species which should never have been kept together with Discus: for example, *Barbus tetrazona*, Tiger Barbs, which continuously chase the Discus fish; and *Uaru amphiacanthoides*, Uarus, which though a lovely cichlid, never allows any Discus fish to get enough food. One of the strangest combination of fish I have ever seen was in Ocean Park in Bangkok, Thailand, where some German-bred fully grown Turquoise Discus were being kept with a number of fancy Goldfish. I believe that this aquarium, inspite of the unorthodox combination of fish, was very successful.

The choice of companion fish must rest with the hobbyist; but it is always a good idea to have only one or two other varieties, but in large numbers. One of the most successful mixed furnished aqua-riums I have ever kept contained 10 fully grown Turquoise Discus fish with several thousand *Cheirodon axelrodi*, Cardinal Tetras: these Tetras, with their striking colours and markings and shoaling movement, complemented the Discus to such an extent, that after a while, one could not imagine the one without the other.

Another lovely combination would be a number of Discus fish with a shoal of *Phenacogrammus interruptus*, Congo Tetras.

Pterophyllum-altum, the Altum Angel fish; no Angel fish should ever be kept with Discus.

Phenacogrammus interruptus, Congo Tetra.

Petitella georgiae, Red-nose Tetra, another suitable companion fish for the mixed, furnished Discus aquarium.

The following fish are suitable for the mixed aquarium: *Cheirodon axelrodi*, Cardinal Tetra; *Phenacogrammus interruptus*, Congo Tetra; *Petitella georgiae*, Red-nose Tetra; many of the *Hemigrammus* family; *Botia macracantha*, Clown Loach; *Microgeophagus ramirezi*, Rainbow Cichlid or Ram; or even *Kryptopterus bicirrhis*, the Ghost fish.

All the fish go well with Discus fish in a display aquarium but one should make sure always to have a shoal of at least 10 or 20 of these fish otherwise they often become very shy, and the desired effect is completely lost. Also, the well-being of

the Discus fish must always be the chief consideration.

A small shoal of any of the Tetras will also help to keep the water clean, by eating up all the very small pieces of food that the Discus fish generally ignore. They also often help new Discus fish to settle in much more quickly.

As most aquarists also like to keep some kind of catfish in their furnished mixed aquariums, because they will keep the substrate somewhat cleaner, some Clown Loaches would be the most suitable. They make very effective scavengers; they are happy in the high water temperature that the Discus need and are very tolerant of the hardness and pH value of the water.

I have never been really successful with any catfish of the *Corydoras* family for any length of time; although they can normally be kept at the Discus aquarium temperature, I found that they never seemed to last very long. In a Discus aquarium, the pH value of the water sometimes drops to a very low level, which is still tolerated by the Discus fish, but never by the *Corydoras*.

Catfish of the *Hypostomus* or *Plecostomus* family are also not suitable, because they eventually grow too large, and because of their nocturnal habit.

When the lighting is off over the aquarium, the Discus fish will settle down in a corner, and will hardly move until daybreak; in the meantime, these suckermouth catfish will scavenge the aquarium, not only disturbing the Discus, but often also sticking to their sides. I have often seen big suction marks on fully grown Discus fish.

A suitable type of suckermouth catfish is the Clown *Plecostomus* which grows to not more than 7 cm in length and also the *Ancistrus* catfish, which also does not exceed 6 to 7 cm. These fish seem to fit well into the furnished mixed aquarium and are recommended.

Botia macracantha, the Clown Loach, a 'catfish' well suited for the Discus fish aquarium.

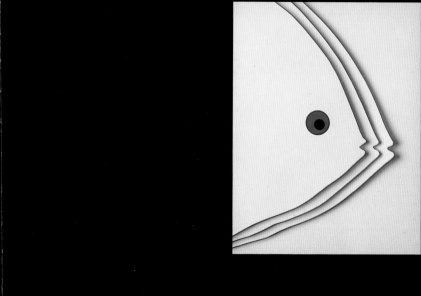

INTRODUCING DISCUS FISH INTO A FURNISHED AQUARIUM

A happy group of Discus in a partly furnished aquarium.

As I said earlier, it can be very frustrating for the hobbyist to see his Discus fish not taking readily to their new environment. This is likely to happen when plenty of hiding places have been provided under bogwood roots or rocks or amongst the live plants. As Discus fish are naturally very shy, they will certainly make use of any cover that there is.

When the transfer is done too quickly, into badly prepared water, the fish are bound to be even more stressed than being moved would normally make them. In all probability, they will then hide for several days. The hobbyist who at this point tries to bring them out by poking a net or scraper at them, is certainly not going to improve the situation.

If Discus fish are young fish, they will settle in much quicker than adults; after a day or two, the first one will appear when food is given. A few hours later, another one will have found enough courage to join in, and with luck, in another day or so, all the Discus will behave as though they had never been moved. Even now, they may take fright for no apparent reason, but should soon be back at the front glass, waiting to be fed. To ease the frustration at this point it is a good idea to introduce into the aquarium a number of the other fish chosen to be companions to the Discus. If they are put into the aquarium at the same time as the Discus fish, this should certainly help to shorten the settling-in period.

With adolescent or adult Discus, settling in can be even longer and more frustrating. Discus fish have been known to hide for as long as three weeks without moving from their place or taking any food at all. Then one day one of them will come to the front glass as though nothing had ever happened; and within a few hours all the other fish will also suddenly start behaving as though they had always been in this aquarium. After this, the fish may never again return to their first hiding place. These settling-in periods are one of the Discus fancier's most frustrating experiences.

There is another way of getting a Discus fish accustomed to a furnished aquarium. It works much better, and makes the fish much less shy. This method reverses the common practice of

first setting up the aquarium, with gravel, plants, decorations etc., letting it run in for a week or so, and then introducing the fish.

The aquarium is filled with water, and the heater/thermostat is used to bring the water to the right temperature. Water conditioners are added to make the water safe, and the filtration systems are installed. Then the fish are put in. As the aquarium is unfurnished, the fish have nowhere to hide, and should settle in very quickly and start to behave normally in a day or so.

Once they have started to feed well, an oxydator can then be put into the aquarium. This will encourage the initial growth of aerobic bacteria, often preventing the sudden build-up of nitrite which is quite usual at this time, because

their final position. If the fish continue to take no notice, then after several more days, some more pieces of bogwood or rocks can be added. If the Discus fish are each time given another few days or a week to get used to their new surroundings, the aquarium can be gradually planted up with medium-sized and background plants.

If for some reason the fish suddenly

the filtration does not become fully effective for several weeks. The oxydator, being small, will not give the fish enough cover, and will be ignored.

After a week or so, some of the smaller types of foreground plants can be put into position. Again, experience shows that the fish will ignore them. A week later, some of the prepared pieces of bogwood or rocks can be introduced and put into

decide to hide under any of the cover, the hiding-places can always be removed, and put back into position a week later. Rarely, though, should this be necessary. By using this 'reverse' method, and working slowly, the fishkeeper will have a fully furnished display aquarium without the frustration so often experienced. It may take a little longer but the result is certainly worth it.

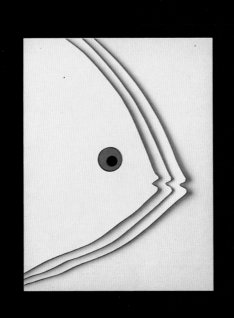

THE OPTIMUM DISCUS FISH AQUARIUM

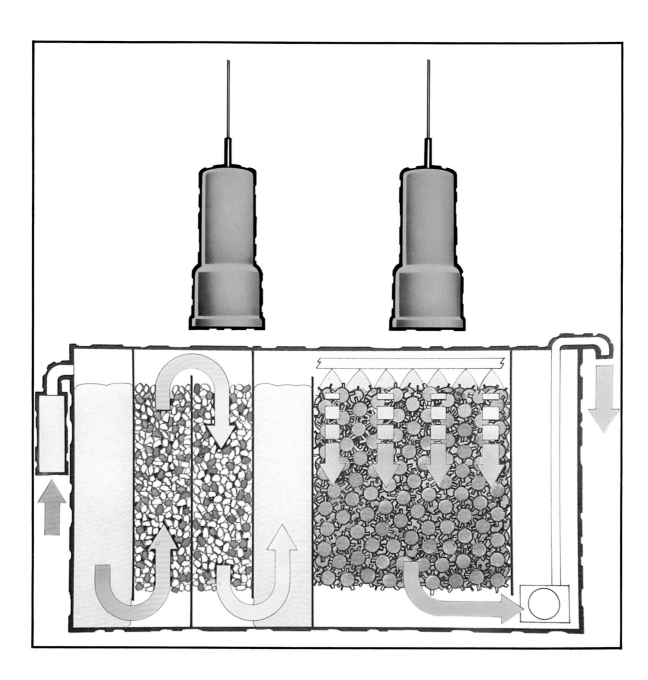

The optimum Discus fish aquarium is a single integral system measuring 130 cm in length by 60 cm in depth by 50 cm in height. It can be either all-glass or the fully framed kind. It has a built-in filtration system, consisting of a pre-filter, a fine pre-filter chamber, two bio-chambers, a pre-trickle chamber, a trickle chamber and a pump-housing chamber. The overall size of the filtering unit is 100 cm x 12.5 cm x 45 cm (length x depth x height). Even allowing for the thickness of the glass partitions, the compartments are of a comfortable size.

The first chamber is filled with a fine pre-filtering material and measures approximately 10 cm x 12.5 cm x 45 cm. The second and third chambers are of the same size; they are filled with biological materials. The pre-trickle chamber is filled with peat, charcoal or some fine post-filtering material such as wadding, to keep the trickle filter clean. It also measures approximately 10 cm x 12.5 cm x 45 cm.

Hi-fin Turquoise Discus.

The trickle chamber is filled with any suitable trickle filtering material, like Dupla's Bioballs, ICI's Flocor RS Biomedia or plastic hair-rollers. A close-fitting perforated sheet is placed above the filtering material, so that the water is distributed evenly over the whole area.

The trickle chamber measures approximately 46.5 x 12.5 cm x 45 cm. The pump-housing chamber only contains either a rotary or a centrifugal pump, to lift the water back into the aquarium.

In the filtering operation, the water passes into the fine pre-filter chamber through an easily serviced pre-filter inside the aquarium, about 5 cm below water level. All suspended dirt particles are caught by the pre-filter, which must be cleaned as often as seems necessary. The water then passes into the fine pre-filter chamber, where even finer particles of suspended matter are retained.

The water rises through the first bio-chamber, and down into the second bio-chamber. Bacteria, both aerobic and anaerobic settle in the bio-chambers, and there the first stage of biological purification takes place.

The water then rises up through the pre-trickle chamber, where any minute particles of dirt or dissolved matter are retained, and then falls onto the perforated screen and spread evenly over the whole area of the trickle chamber. It then drops onto the filtering material, where the established nitrifying bacteria convert most of the dissolved substances into relatively harmless matter. The large amount of oxygen needed by the bacteria is taken from the atmosphere and the trickle filter is almost self-cleaning, requiring very little maintenance. Dead bacteria are washed away and collect in the pump chamber, from which they must be siphoned once in a while. Finally, the water rises into the pump chamber, and is returned to the main aquarium by either the rotary or centrifugal pump.

Angled glass partitions are attached with silicone sealant to both the front corners of the aquarium, and to convenient places on the filtering unit. In the two partitioned-off sections, a selection of suitable, fast-growing plants are then planted in a medium containing iron. The water passes and returns from these planted sections into the main aquarium either through holes provided, or on the overflow principle.

Above the two planted sections, mercury vapour or miniature metal halide spots are installed to ensure an intense light for the plants. Because of this, the plants grow vigorously, not only providing an oxygen-rich water, but also helping to remove toxins from the water. Regular feeding of the plants with iron, other trace elements and carbon dioxide ensures a luscious plant growth, resulting in a biologically balanced aquarium.

The temperature of the water in the optimum Discus fish aquarium is controlled by an electronic thermostat, which gives precise and easily adjustable

control. A heating source is installed in the planted section: either a glass heater, or a low-voltage undergravel heater. The aquarium holds approximately 380 litres of water, and requires a 175-watt heating element if it is kept in a warm room, and 350-watt if it is kept in a cold room.

The water for the optimum Discus aquarium will have a carbonate hardness of 4 dH, a total hardness of 8 dH and a pH value of 6.6 to 6.8. The temperature of the water will be maintained at 29°C.

The overhead lights are controlled by a time-switch. During the first week, the plants need approximately 6 hours of lighting; this is increased by two hours in the second week, and by a further two hours in the third week. A final adjustment is made after this time, and depends on the types of plants used, as well as on the light sources and their position.

The Discus fish are kept and looked after in the angled open section. This is the 'clinical' part of the optimum aquarium, where any uneaten food or accumulated waste can clearly be seen and removed. This section can house five fully-grown Discus fish, or up to 10 medium-sized specimens. They will behave more confidently and grow faster than fish kept in other sorts of installations, because of the efficiency of the filtration; because of the beneficial effect of the growing plants on the water quality; and because of the ease of maintenance.

The gravel of the plant sections needs no maintenance at all, and the plants themselves need only occasional pruning, to keep them from choking through their own abundant growth. The pre-filter must be regularly inspected, and changed as soon as it needs it; and any uneaten food and waste products should be siphoned out every day, and the water replaced in the aquarium. If this is done, there should be no real need for a weekly change of water. The optimum Discus fish aquarium is, consequently, superlatively easy to maintain.

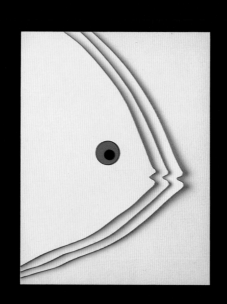

BREEDING

Schmidt-Focke bred Red Turquoise with wriggling larvae on oxydator.

Probably every Discus fish keeper dreams of being one day successful in breeding these fish. This ambition may not be easy to fulfil.

In the past, the keeping of Discus used to be beset with many difficulties, which are now better understood, and known to be related either to unsuitable environmental conditions, or to diseases. Almost all of these diseases can now be treated, with the help of modern drugs; and many water analyses that have been published of the Discus fish's natural habitat have enabled aquarists to keep these fish in perfect health, without any need for guesswork.

Yet it is a different story when it comes to getting the fish to breed: in spawning, they very often defy rational expectations. In theory, any mature pair of Discus fish should be able to spawn: in practice, this just isn't so.

With wild-caught Discus the female fish is usually the more willing partner, and with an attentive male, will spawn within a week or so. Amongst the males, however, it is only the 'dominant' one that will show any signs of being interested in a willing female and spawn in a relatively short time. The 'hangers on' sometimes take as long as 6 to 10 months to be aroused to sexual activity. I have observed this over many years, and it seems to be the rule rather than the exception. There are also some Discus fish, both female and male, which will never spawn, however good their condition or environment.

Some Discus fish will spawn almost continuously for one keeper, but not for another. Some years ago I had a very prolific breeding pair of *Symphysodon aequifasciata haraldi*. The male was fully striated and showed intense coloration. The female was equally intensely coloured but showed the striation on only about 80% of the body; the majority of the offspring carried the colour and markings of the male. The average size of the brood was almost always more than 150 young. The parent fish could only have been described as an ideal pair. Reluctantly I sold them to an American friend who was then living in London. He kept these fish in an aquarium of an identical size to mine, with identical water conditions, filtration, etc. but was unable to get them to spawn. After six months or so, these fish were returned to me; and they spawned within a few hours, in a hospital tank which was certainly too small, containing not more than 60 litres of water. It was also very shallow, and it was obvious that the fish had difficulty in laying the eggs in vertical rows against the back pane of the aquarium.

A quick telephone call brought the totally amazed and flabbergasted American back to my premises, to watch what he had waited in vain to see in his own aquarium, during the previous six months. He collected the parents again when the fry was ready to be moved, and once more installed them in his tank. We checked and double-checked every single item in his set-up, only to find that it in no way differed from mine. These fish again failed to spawn for my friend during the next five months.

When he was later transferred to Washington DC, he asked me to send these fish to him, once he was settled in his new home. After being in a bag for many hours, and enduring an arduous journey across the Atlantic, the fish spawned within two days of arrival and reared their young. I cannot offer any sensible explanation at all for these events, but they remain an attested fact.

During the last 20 years or so I have sold many 'proven' breeding pairs of Discus fish to hobbyists in many countries of the world. I have also conducted what must rank as one of the strangest Discus fish transactions: I have supplied a hobbyist in Rio de Janeiro, Brazil, with Brazilian wild-caught Discus from London, England. Most of the breeding pairs I have sold have fulfilled their potential; but there have been occasions when a proven breeding pair was unwilling to spawn for the new owner. Although the chances of success are very high, no one could ever give an unconditional guarantee.

It is generally agreed nowadays that the best way of improving ones chances of breeding Discus is to start with a number of either young or adolescent fish: well-cared for Discus fish are generally sexually mature at about 12 months, give or take a few weeks.

With a number of fish in one aquarium, one can be sure at least of having both males and females, although there is still no guarantee that the fish will pair off. If there is no sign of any pairing off, the fish could be moved to other tanks until they themselves find partners.

This breeding pair was fed daily with shrimp eggs. Even the eggs take on a more red coloration than is usually normal.

In most cases, however, nature will take its course. After many, sometimes quite vicious fights, in which the fish often show all their vertical bars, and the coloration of the body becomes almost black, the potential breeding pair will separate themselves from the rest of the community, and settle down in one of the corners of the aquarium. They will then almost always stay together and defend their territory. There may still be the occasional skirmish, but seldom as fierce

as before. This almost continuous staying together is a clear sign that the fish have found one another; if they are kept with other fish, they will seldom take part in the activities in the aquarium, such as feeding or fighting. Often, they will also become more reluctant to take food.

The hobbyist must now decide whether the pair or the rest of the fish are to be moved to another aquarium. I have sometimes moved the pair and sometimes the other fish, since I believe that the stress caused to the pair is about the same in each case. If the pair are moved, they will suffer stress and will need a little while to settle down. If, however, it is the remaining fish that are moved, trying to catch them in the tank will also disturb the pair, which will again need some time to settle. In either case, the settling should only take a few days.

At this point the hobbyist must introduce a suitable spawning substrate. This can be a piece of slate angled against the side or back of the aquarium, or a clay flower-pot inverted in the centre, or even an oxydator. The fish seem to prefer a rather somewhat rough surface. However, even though provided with several spawning substrates, the fish may in the end decide to spawn against the glass, against the intake pipe of a power filter, or even on the heating element. It is therefore important to have as little clutter in the aquarium as possible, and to position the power filter intake pipe and the heater in such a way that they cannot easily be used as a breeding substrate. If the fish decide to spawn against any of the sides of the aquarium, there is very little the hobbyist can do.

Once the Discus fish have chosen a particular spot, they may hover around it for some time, which may be days or even weeks, staring continuously at the spot, but showing no apparent signs of sexual activity.

At this point the fish should be fed on a variety of foods; the filtration system should be at its most efficient, and the quality of the water should be carefully checked, and any necessary alterations carried out. If the fish show no signs of willingness to spawn, a large water change of approximately 30% will often trigger off sexual activity. It is important though, that the temperature and composition of the fresh water should be similar.

Often after such a water change the fish will suddenly become more active. They will bow to one another while swimming past. This will be followed by a gentle shaking of the body, gradually increasing in frequency, duration and vigour. With some breeding pairs, this activity may continue for several days, or sometimes even weeks, whereas with other pairs, it may be hardly noticeable, and take no longer than a few hours.

Next comes the mouthing stage. The female is usually the initiator, and will return to the chosen spawning site, mouthing it as though to clean it. Occasionally she will swim towards the male, bow, shake, and return to continue the cleaning. In a well-matched pair, the male will follow the female, and also start cleaning. The shaking will continue until spawning has been completed. The mouthing or cleaning of the spawning site will normally take several hours. Sometimes a second site is sought, which may, in the end, not be used at all.

Mr. Kanok Kiattorn, manager in charge of Discus breeding for Star Aquarium, Bangkok, Thailand.

For a long time it was thought that the mouthing of the breeding substrate was in fact a way of cleaning it, freeing it from algae or other dirt. But fish that have been provided with a completely clean spawning substrate will also go through the same ritual. Whether the mouthing is part of the pre-spawning activity, or whether the fish actually deposit a secretion on the site on which to lay the eggs, has so far not been established.

At this stage, just before spawning, the breeding pair undergoes a colour change. The body becomes much darker, the dorsal fins become almost jet-black, but the colour of the head becomes much lighter than that of non-breeding Discus.

As the activity around the spawning site becomes more vigorous, it should become possible to distinguish the sexes. The breeding tube in both the female and the male will become clearly visible; in the female, it will greatly protrude from the body, sometimes as much as 3 to 4 mm, and will be blunt, whereas the breeding tube of the male will be considerably shorter and thinner, and will come to a point.

SPAWNING

After a number of 'trial runs' by the female at the spawning substrate, often with an occasional mouthing in between, she will start to deposit her eggs on the substrate. The eggs are deposited upwards in single rows, five to twelve at the time. In shallow tanks, or with too small a breeding substrate, the eggs may be laid almost horizontally. After the female has laid the eggs, the male will swim over them, depositing his sperm. With some pairs the two activities will happen simultaneously. This sequence of events will take about one hour, by which time all the eggs will have been laid and fertilized. The number of eggs will greatly depend on the age and condition of the female; the older the female, the fewer the eggs; there may be as few as 30 or as many as 250, but the average seems to be around 100.

Spawning usually takes place in the late afternoon or early evening. It is seldom that spawning takes place at any other time. I have witnessed many spawnings, not just in England and Europe, but

able to change the fish's breeding pattern. Although many suggestions were forthcoming, no satisfactory explanation of this phenomenon has so far been offered.

Once the laying of the eggs is finished, the pair will guard the clutch, and continuously fan the eggs with their pectoral

also in many parts of the Far East. Discus fish in Europe usually spawn at the onset of darkness, and also do the same in the Far East, in spite of the time difference. Their 'built-in clock' seems to be able to adjust easily to the time differences.

However, this seems to have little to do with the failing light. Several years ago I carried out an experiment with several breeding pairs which regularly spawned at a given time. In a completely darkened fish-house, which daylight could not enter, I changed the light setting by 12 hours, and changed the hours of feeding and maintenance accordingly. The fish continued to spawn at their previous regular time. I continued this experiment for almost six months, without ever being

fins. This supplies the eggs with oxygen-rich water and at the same time removes dirt particles. The colour of the fish will remain darker; some breeding pairs will now have almost reverted to normal though some fish retain the breeding coloration much longer than others. The dorsal fins will be almost jet-black, and the colour of the head will always be much lighter now than in non-breeding Discus fish. At a temperature of 29 to 30°C, the eggs will hatch in approximately 55 to 60 hours.

AFTER HATCHING

Once the eggs have hatched, the parents suck them out of their eggshells, mouth them and spit them on to the breeding substrate. The larvae are attached to the breeding substrate by glands on their heads which secrete a mucous substance. After a while, a great black mass of larvae can be seen wriggling and being guarded by the parents. If any of the larvae should wriggle itself free of the substrate, it is usually picked up by one of the parents before it can sink all the way to the bottom of the aquarium. The German type of clay breeding cone, with its gentle sloping sides and several protruding rims, is best for catching the falling fry before it sinks.

When all the larvae have hatched out, usually within four to five hours, the parents usually move them to another site. This may be a few centimetres from the original spot, or it may be on the other side of the aquarium, but it is sure to be a place where the hobbyist will have the greatest difficulty in observing the larvae. If they are not moved within the first 24 hours, then they will usually not be moved at all. During this period, they obtain their food from their egg sac, which can clearly be seen. They become free-swimming after a further 60 to 70 hours, depending on the temperature of the water.

It is at this time that the parents become very busy. As soon as one fry makes his first attempt at independence, the parents quickly chase after it, suck it in their mouths, and spit it back on to the clutch. More and more fry make their first attempt at free-swimming; after a short while, it becomes quite obvious that the parents can no longer cope with chasing after every single fry. One of the fish (more often than not the female) then positions itself very near the hatched-out young, so that they can swim straight on to its body, while the other fish continues to chase after the fugitive larvae to bring them back. At this stage, they are no longer spat onto the breeding substrate, but are released near the nursing fish. Within an hour or so, all the fry can be

seen 'grazing' from the sides of the parents; they are taking their first real food, slime secreted by the parents' bodies.

A new type of food, suitable as a supplement for the first week or so, has now become available from Germany, where it is produced by AB Aquatechnik. It is called Aquabiofood U, and consists of eight amino acids, two fats, two carbohydrates and eight vitamins. The makers claim that due to the balanced composition of the food, and the resulting total absorption, there is practically no excretion, and therefore the water stays free of waste matter.

I have used this food supplement for several years now with all my breeding stock, and have found that the fry do actually grow much faster with it than they do without it. In fact, I start feeding Aquabiofood U as soon as the eggs hatch out, when they are still in a cluster on the breeding substrate.

To begin with, I use a syringe to squirt the liquid food, a few drops at the time, over the wriggling larvae. I have found that by starting while the fry are still neatly clustered together, I need to use less food, and the fry obviously get used to it faster. Later, when they are free-swimming, they will actually swim into the food cloud; and also the parent fish have by then accepted the squirting procedure. However, if the food is given for the first time when the fry are already free-swimming, many of them will disperse, and much of the benefit will be lost.

I continue to use this food supplement at least three to four times a day for the first week or so. After 72 hours, when the fry are free-swimming, the food is squirted on the sides of the nursing fish, from which the fry take it with the body slime.

I have never used Aquabiofood U to rear baby Discus fish artificially, because I have never needed to do so. From contact with other Discus fish breeders I know that some of them have had great success using this method, while others have failed miserably. Whether this was because of the food, or because of some other factor, such as pollution, I cannot at present say.

The feeding from the parents' secretion is almost continuous, and a dim light should be left on above the aquarium for 24 hours a day during the first few weeks at least. Sometimes only one of the parent fish has all the fry, while at other times they are shared. The fry are transferred from one fish to the other by a quick push forward. The parents are alongside each other; then one, with a quick jerk releases all the fry, which remain momentarily suspended in the water, and then swim to the sides of the other fish.

At this stage, the fry never wander more than a few centimetres from the parents. Because of the continuous feeding, their stomachs are always full and round. After the first five or six days, the fry become a little bit more adventurous, and wander a little bit further from the security of the parents. If anybody approaches the aquarium, the parents signal danger by twitching, and the fry return to their sides and remain there motionless, until the parents start to behave normally again. Even though the fry may be very close to them, the adults will continue twitching until the danger seems to have passed. This 'danger' may be nothing more than somebody staring into the aquarium, doing a little maintenance or even feeding the fish.

After five to six days or so, it is common practice in Europe and America to give the fish newly-hatched brine shrimps. The nauplii of the *Artemia* are hatched out in a brine solution, which takes about 24 hours. The hobbyist is advised to have at least three or four such cultures on the go, set up at four-hourly intervals, in order to have a constant supply. The shrimps must be rinsed in clean water before being given to the fish. The first and often also second time that these baby shrimps are fed to the fry, they will be ignored. As they can easily pollute the water, any uneaten shrimps should be siphoned from the aquarium within the hour.

Once the fry have got used to this new food, it should be given as often as possible. It is better to give small quantities ten times a day, than larger amounts only five times a day. Even the small quantities create a 'cloud' of shrimps and the fry very quickly learn to swim into it. The red coloration of their stomachs is a clear indication of how much they are eating and often it seems though their stomachs were about to burst.

During the night, with a dim light still on above the aquarium, the fry will continue to feed off the parents. During the first two weeks of life, the fry, if properly fed, should, at the very least, quadruple in size.

In the Far East, especially in Thailand, Discus fry are fed, as early as the second or third day, with minute crustaceans. These tiny red *Daphnia*-like creatures are given in great quantities and produce a fast growth rate: the fry reach a size of 1 cm in the first six days of free-swimming. I have never known fry fed any other type of food to grow as fast as this. These crustaceans are now imported into England, deep-frozen, and have been successfully used in rearing many batches of fry.

Many hobbyists have suffered some losses among fry that were fed wholly on the brine shrimps, because of the salt content. Fry will grow just as fast on the imported crustaceans, and with hardly any losses.

When the fish have reached a size when these tiny foods are too small to eat, the hobbyist must find several alternatives. Some of these could be: a prepared food consisting mainly of oxheart, blended with vitamins, etc.; shrimp eggs from the freshwater shrimp *Macrobrachium rosenbergii*, which is now generally available deep-frozen; black

This pair had to be separated; the 3 day old fry can easily swim through the wire-mesh partition and feed of both parents.

or red Mosquito larvae. As long as the food is prepared in a size that the young fish can take, and offered in variety, the fish will continue to grow. Under no circumstances should live *Tubifex* be given.

When the fish are two to three weeks old, they can be moved to their own aquarium. Fry left with the parents for a while longer do seem to grow rather better; but there comes a point at which the fry continue to nibble at the parents' sides, when they no longer need to, causing them actual damage. When this happens, the fry must be moved to their own quarters. With good feeding, the fry will have reached a size of about 2.5 to 3 cm by two months, and can be cared for like any other young Discus fish.

WHEN THINGS GO WRONG

If the account I have just given of Discus fish breeding were the norm, the fish would probably have nothing like the same attraction for hobbyists. I am sure that many of them are attracted to Discus not only because of their sheer beauty, coloration and size, but because of the great difficulties in propagation. Hobbyists often need a challenge: it was because of such a challenge that I, more than 20 years ago, started to become interested in these fish. I was told then that I would not be able to keep them

alive for longer than three months, much less breed them. I have stayed with these fish ever since!

As I already mentioned earlier, there are some fish that will not breed under any circumstances. The likelihood of having such a fish is not very great, but there will sometimes be one in a group of five or six. No one knows why such fish occur. They refuse to mate even with the most easy going, over-sexed partner. They may be so set upon or bullied by other fish, that they have to be rescued. Unfortunately, these fish seem almost to be particularly beautiful, but they are really only useful as an addition to a display aquarium.

Then there are those pairs which have spawned on previous occasions but are suddenly no longer willing to do so. A fertile pair are capable of spawning almost every week or so for several months. The intervals are sometimes as short as four days, but may be as long as two weeks. The frequency greatly depends on the condition of the fish and their environment, as well as their food. If the fish are kept in proper conditions, they will spawn at shorter intervals than fish kept in less favourable conditions.

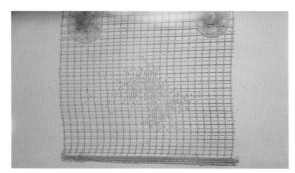

Eggs laid on the back glass of the aquarium being protected with a wire-mesh.

If the fish show no signs of mating after having had a 'rest period' for several months, the established procedure is to introduce a third fish into the aquarium. This often re-vitalizes the pairs' breeding instinct, but may also cause great stress to the third fish. I have never yet been able to find a fish that will stimulate the pair without being severely damaged. If the third fish is somewhat more aggressive and stands its ground, then it usually does not have the desired effect on the pair. The recurrent fights amongst the fish result only in damage to the pair, as well as to the third fish.

If the pair has previously been a good pair, then the third fish should not be kept too long in their company. If the 'third-fish method' is going to work at all, it will show results within a few days, and the third fish can be removed before too much damage has been done.

This method can also be used with the third fish separated from the pair by a glass partition or a wire-mesh partition; it can even be kept in an adjoining tank. The third fish will then not be harmed, but often one of the pair will have a damaged nose from swimming furiously against the glass. The method I prefer is to have two tanks side by side. This keeps the third fish safe from attack, and an opaque divider can be inserted for part of the day between the two tanks. The stimulating effect is the same, but it can be controlled from the outside by the hobbyist when it gets out of hand.

Sometimes too much interference by the keeper can discourage the fish from spawning. I know from experience that many Discus fish keepers fuss too much with their tanks. I do not advocate neglect: there must be a certain level of daily maintenance, the fish must be fed several times a day, water changes may become necessary; but sometimes there is continual interference, which does not allow the fish to settle down. It may be difficult for any hobbyist to agree to leave the aquarium alone for several weeks, since it was instilled in him that Discus fish need great care and attention. This is, indeed, true, but it must be the right kind of attention.

One way to encourage the fish to spawn is to give them only basic attention for several weeks, feeding them as usual several times a day, but not being too fussy about the waste they produce. So long as the filtration is working well, there should be no risk of a nitrite build-up, or even denitrification. It does not even matter if the front glass of the tank becomes so opaque that the fish can hardly be seen. Then after three or four weeks, there should be a large water change of 50 to 70 %, using water with a slightly different hardness and pH value. This method often stimulates the fish into spawning.

A few years ago, I supplied a great number of various fish bred in Germany by Dr. E. Schmidt-Focke, to a hobbyist in the Far East. I was able to see these fish a year later. Some of them were kept in a breeding establishment, where they were given water changes twice a day, and although they had grown to their full size, their coloration was rather disappointing. The rest of the fish were kept in several tanks in an apartment; these had been neglected during a vacation and the owner was almost too embarrassed to show me the fish because of the state of the tanks. The others looked much more like the fish I had known, with their strong colorations and markings. After I left the Far East, I was told that some of these pairs had spawned within three or four days of being given a large water change. If there is basically nothing wrong with either the fish or their environment, this method is often successful.

It sometimes happens that the fish lay eggs but they always grow fungus within a day or two. This may mean that one or the other of the pair may not be fertile; or that the 'pair' are, in fact, two females; or that the water is polluted and burdened with bacteria.

If fish become temporarily infertile, this may be the result of a poor diet, lacking vitamins, or of a lack of trace elements in the water. Eggs easily grow fungus in water that is too new and not yet biologically stable; with time the aquarium will become mature and eggs will begin to hatch out. Also, Discus fish become temporarily infertile after the application of certain medicines. When treated with *Metronidazole*, for instance, the fish will need at least four to six weeks before the drug leaves their system and they are again capable of producing fertile eggs and sperm. It is thought, that certain broad-spectrum antibacterial medicines have a similar effect, although the Discus fish seem to recover from them much sooner.

A pair of fish may turn out to be two females, in spite of a visible difference between their breeding tubes. Not every female has a breeding tube of the same size; if one breeding tube should be extra large and the other extra small, one could be easily fooled into thinking that the fish were of two different sexes.

Very occasionally it happens that two females lay eggs simultaneously on the same substrate, but to no effect. This can happen even in a display aquarium, in the presence of males. In such cases, the hobbyist should try pairing the females with males known to be capable.

Eggs will grow fungus when the water condition is not right, because of a high bacterial count, or the water is biologically unstable, lacking in humic and other organic substances. Water of the

Turquoise female with 'protected' eggs.

right kind is certainly the most important factor not only in the general well-being of the Discus fish but also in their successful propagation. Even if some of the other conditions are not absolutely right, the fish will spawn and rear some fry, though perhaps only a few. But if the quality of the water is not within a certain range, the breeder is bound to fail.

When the discrepancies are slight, they can easily be corrected by a more effective biological filtration, by the use of ozone or ultra-violet sterilization, or by an anti-fungus remedy. I myself, as a matter of course, use a product called Cilex, manufactured in West Germany by Brustmann: one of its active ingredients is acriflavine. It is a specific breeding aid, for preventing eggs from going mouldy. If the water conditions are really unsuitable, it will have no effect, but if they are only slightly out, it will stop the eggs from going mouldy, so that they will hatch out. By using one tablet per 15 to 20 litres of water, any small bacterial condition can be kept in check. The water will take on a fluorescent yellow-green tint, which will become paler each day, as it is destroyed by light. Even if it remains in the water, it will in no way affect the eggs or sperm of any subsequent spawning.

Then there are the egg eaters. These fish will do everything right: they will have their pre-spawning ritual, they will clean and mouth the spawning substrate, they will often also be very gentle to each other, which is always a sign of a well-matched pair; the female will deposit her eggs; and instead of fertilizing them with his breeding tube, the male will eat every single one. I once had a male which with one particular female would always eat the eggs as soon as they were laid. When this fish was given another female, the egg eating suddenly stopped. In the end, he became quite a good, attentive parent with most females.

There are those fish which will look after the eggs in the normal fashion for a while, only to eat them later, sometimes just a few hours before they were due to hatch. Then there are pairs, one of which claims the exclusive right of looking after the eggs. At the beginning, there may only be minor squabbles; later, they become fiercer, and one fish is continually driven away by the other from the breeding substrate. The eggs are sure to be eaten before the time of hatching out. Nobody knows why certain Discus fish are such notorious egg eaters. Many experiments have been carried out to find an answer. It has been suggested that Discus fish eat their eggs simply because of hunger, but this must surely be the most unlikely reason.

Sometimes though, a habitual egg eater abandons the habit, and never eats another egg. This is what happened in England with a particular male Discus fish, which ate 96 spawning one after the other, and then never touched another one.

So far, egg eating has been mentioned only in connections with males; but sometimes it is the female that eat the eggs.

One way of making it more difficult for the eggs to be eaten is to shield them with a wire mesh. The parents can still look after the eggs but are prevented from getting too close to them; and with any luck, by the time the eggs are ready to hatch out, the fish may have developed a stronger parental instinct. When trying to breed for the first time with a young, inexperienced Discus fish, it is advisable to match it with a 'seasoned' partner, so that it will not get into egg-eating habits.

It becomes even more frustrating when the eggs hatch out, but the parents suddenly decide to eat the larvae. In such cases there is very little that can be done. Occasionally, these fish stop this habit after several spawning and will rear any subsequent broods. If they do not stop, however, then the fry will have to be reared artificially. Detailed accounts of the procedure can be found in *All about*

Discus by Dr. Herbert R. Axelrod, and in *Handbook of Discus* by Jack Wattley. Both of these books are published by TFH of America.

Another problem which sometimes arises is that the fry cannot find the parents even though mucous on the sides of the fish is clearly visible. They seem to swim aimlessly through the aquarium, sometimes only centimetres away from the parents, without attaching themselves to their sides. It may be that in such cases there is something wrong with the mucous. These fry will die within a few hours, because of the lack of their first food. Artificial rearing of such fry seems to be the only answer.

Another critical stage seems to be when the baby fish have been free-swimming for about two weeks, and have been fed for one week on newly-hatched brine shrimps. For no apparent reason, a small number of fish may die each day. It used to be thought that the fish had choked on the shells of the *Artemia*; but the same thing happens when shell-less *Artemia* are used. I am convinced that the baby fish die because of the accumulated salt content from the *Artemia*, and the hobbyist should wash the newly-hatched brine shrimps thoroughly in fresh water.

This problem can be almost completely eliminated by using some other food. Hobbyists use these brine shrimps as a first food for many different kinds of fish, but it seems that these inexplicable deaths only occur among Discus fish fry.

The final critical stage in the development of the fry usually happens when the fish are four to five weeks old. Again, a small number of fish will die each day without any outward signs of ill-health. This is usually the result of bad water management. The aquarium and filtration will have been heavily burdened during the previous four to five weeks; the filtration has suddenly had to cope with a large additional amount of food, much of it decomposed. In the Far East,

where large daily water changes are customary, heavy feeding never makes the water foul, even without filtration, and there seems to be no problems with the baby Discus fish at this stage of their development.

MAINTENANCE IN A BREEDING TANK

I am often asked whether maintenance should be halted in an aquarium with eggs, larvae or very young fry. My answer has always been the same: no fish is ever harmed by the addition of fresh, clean water.

The reluctance of some hobbyists to carry out partial water changes during this period is perhaps understandable. They are afraid that the parents will, as a result, eat the eggs or even the larvae. There is really no reason to believe that this might happen because of changing the water, cleaning out the filter, or carefully removing the accumulated dirt particles. If the eggs or larvae are eaten by the parents at this stage, they would probably also have been eaten if no maintenance had been done. As I just said, there are breeders in the Far East who, regardless of eggs, larvae or young fry, change up to 90 % of the water twice a day. It goes without saying that the 'new' water must be biologically stable and of the right hardness, pH value and temperature. Some breeders in Germany have as many as four different filters on every breeding tank; each day one of these is cleaned, with the other three remaining biologically active.

The accumulated dirt should be removed from the aquarium within one hour of feeding; and if the new water is added with a pinched airline tubing over a period of 30 minutes or so, no harm will come to the fry. Although in Britain it is seldom possible to change really large amounts of water every day, the addition of 20 to 30 % of new water has never caused any loss of eggs, larvae or young fry.

CREATING A STRAIN

Any ambitious hobbyist could, by selective breeding, create his own strain. It is a very long and tedious task, not made any easier by the reluctance of some Discus fish to co-operate. A strain, colour or any other characteristics will be 'fixed' after five to six generations after which the young can confidently be expected to carry certain characteristics and features of the parents.

Very briefly, colour inheritance works like this: parents pass on to their offspring colour inheritance factors called genes, one set from each parent. If the parents are of the same coloration, and are both pure-bred, all the offspring will show this coloration. If the parents are of different colours, each offspring will receive a set of genes from each, but one colour will be dominant, and the other recessive, and only the dominant colour will show.

For the sake of example, let as call the dominant colour black, and the recessive colour white. Pure-bred parents of the same coloration (BB × BB or WW × WW) can only produce offspring of their own colour. In the case of BB × WW mating, the offspring will carry the genes of both colours but will show only the dominant colour (BW). If such hybrids should mate, some of them (approximately 25 %) will receive the recessive colour genes from each parent and will be white (WW). The same proportion will receive the dominant genes from each parent, and will be black, but will be hybrids, like the parents (BW):-

```
WW  ×  WW  —  WW WW WW WW
BB  ×  WW  —  BW BW BW BW
BW  ×  BW  —  BB BW BW WW
BB  ×  BW  —  BB BB BW BW
WW  ×  BW  —  WW WW BW BW
BB  ×  BB  —  BB BB BB BB
```

With Mendel's theory the foundations of genetics were laid, and all subsequent discoveries are based on his findings. Modern developments in genetic engineering mean that almost any desired characteristics can be produced. Mendel's theory applies to all living

A Singapore Red Turquoise Hi-fin.

things — plants, humans and also fish.

In breeding Discus fish to obtain some particular characteristics, the desired results can be obtained in several ways: line-breeding, using parent fish which are genetically identical to each other and display the same features; by inbreeding, in which brothers are mated with sisters; and by back-crossing where an offspring is mated with one of the parents, father with daughter, or mother with son.

Discus breeders like Dr. E. Schmidt-Focke and Jack Wattley have demonstrated that with selective breeding, many fine colours and features can be achieved. On the other hand, the resulting progeny tend to become smaller and smaller with each generation, deformities are more frequent, the number of eggs decrease, the parental breeding instinct are less developed and the fish are more affected by diseases and environmental conditions. After several generations of selective breeding, the hobbyists must introduce a suitable alternative fish — possibly wild-caught — into his strain, in order to enable it to maintain or regain normal size and other characteristics.

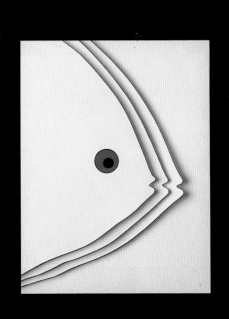

GENERAL MAINTENANCE

At the beginning of this book I said that most hobbyists succeed in keeping and even breeding Discus fish, even with little knowledge, if they have sufficient dedication. This dedication, however, must become a routine. It will not do to attend to the fish when one 'has a minute' or when one 'thinks about it'.

Discus fish are very tolerant; they will not die overnight without first giving warning by their behaviour and colour that something is wrong. And usually it is the environment or the way the fish are looked after that is at fault.

Although one still occasionally comes across the 'old water' theory, it is now generally accepted that the aquarium water must be renewed. How much of the water should be changed at one time depends on many factors; most hobbyists will, within a very short time, get the knack of assessing them. He will ask himself: how efficient is the filtration? Is the aquarium overstocked? Is there an excess of food? All this influences the amount of water to be changed.

There are those who advocate a substantial water change every week or two; others insist on a daily, but smaller, water change. Overall, both methods probably take roughly the same amount of time, but if the condition of the aquarium is to be the chief concern, the daily water change must be the first choice. The addition of 10 to 15 % of fresh water every day keeps the Discus fish in water of constant quality. If 50 % of the water is changed every two weeks only, the water quality deteriorates during this period, and since this is a slow process, the fish get used to it without suffering; however, when the big water change is made, they usually show signs of discomfort because the quality of the water has changed greatly all at once: this is called 'fresh-water shock'.

The filtration also needs constant attention. The pre-filter should be cleaned regularly. If this is done every day, the main filtration not only lasts

much longer, but also becomes more efficient. A complete change of the filtering material should not be carried out at the same time as a large water change, as this would destroy the biological stability of the water. The condition of the aquarium panes is always a good indication of the state of the water. If the glass is covered with a slimy substance, then the water is rich in protein; this indicates the need for larger or more frequent water changes, as well as for a more active filtration unit.

The power unit of the filter must be cleaned from time to time and so must the tubing. The tube connectors and taps as well as the sealing ring must be checked for tightness, to prevent water from seeping out of the system. Uneaten food and faeces must be removed every day, using either a siphon, or a special aquarium 'vacuum cleaner'. The oxydator must be refilled with hydrogen peroxide. The sides of the aquarium should be cleaned with a soft sponge or scraper. All electrical equipment must be checked for safety and proper function.

In a well run-in aquarium the water should be tested twice a week for pH value, oxygen content, and nitrite and nitrate levels, as a check on the condition of the set-up; any necessary changes can be carried out before the fish are in any way affected.

In newly set-up tanks, the tests should

be carried out every day, especially the ones for oxygen and nitrite. A high nitrite reading will be harmful to the fish after a time; so the water must be changed at more frequent intervals, until the filtration system is fully operative. The fresh water should be of the same quality, with the hardness and conductivity as close to identical as possible, though very small changes are tolerated and often act as a stimulant. The pH value must be identical: only very slight changes are tolerated, so great care must be taken.

The water should be conditioned with sodium thiosulphate to remove any chlorine gas; several proprietary products are available, all of which are effective. The water, especially if it is soft, should also be conditioned with trace elements, and with hormones and other biological substances, to give it 'life' and it should also be well oxygenated. A consistent routine, with a consistent water quality must be the aim; this alone can ensure a trouble-free Discus fish aquarium.

By recording all details in a notebook, the hobbyist will soon learn what effect his maintenance has on the system; he will see that certain types of food are less polluting than others, by keeping the pH value of the water more stable. Every detail connected with the fish should be recorded: when they were purchased; their size at the time; their growth rate over a given period of time; health troubles, the medications used and their effectiveness; number of casualties. By clearly recording all these facts, the hobbyist will in the future be able to recognize the symptoms of trouble, and will also know what steps to take and their results.

Many Discus fish disasters can be avoided by having such a notebook to refer to. Such disasters happen both to the novice and to the highly experienced keeper. The novice can be forgiven, as he still has a lot to learn about keeping these fish; but the experienced keeper is often over-confident and ready to take chances with fatal consequences. Yet, had he consulted a notebook, and followed an established procedure, many Discus fish might have been saved.

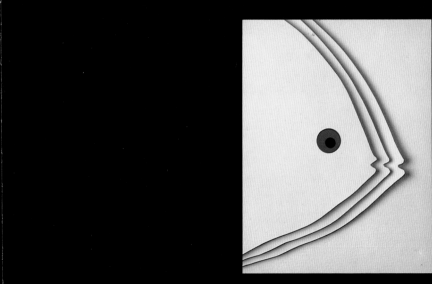

FEEDING AND FOODS

SUITABLE FOODS ● BRINE SHRIMPS ●
DAPHNIA ● RED MOSQUITO LARVAE ●
BLACK MOSQUITO LARVAE ●
WHITEWORMS ● GLASSWORMS ● LIVE
TUBIFEX ● EARTHWORMS ● DEEP-FROZEN
FOOD ● FLAKE, PELLETED AND TABLET
FOOD ● PREPARED FOOD ● VITAMINS

Next to the quality of the water, the variety of the Discus fish food is the most important consideration, yet most hobbyists seem to neglect this side somewhat. They usually opt for the lazy way out, and provide a diet of some live food and prepared oxheart. Although the fish can be sustained on this, they will never reach their full potential; neither will fish which are fed only twice a day.

Some years ago it used to be said that Discus fish were very finicky with their food, and would sooner starve to death, than eat a food they were not used to. Many articles were published in fish-keeping magazines in Europe as well as America, describing the plight of such 'hunger-strikers'. Today, we know better: those fish refused some particular food, not because they did not like it, but they were suffering from some disease. Once this was recognized, the Discus fish, when restored to health, suddenly were found to be avid feeders, willing to take not just the usual live foods, but even prepared foods. A healthy Discus fish is almost continuously looking for food, and will almost eat anything.

Very young fish should be fed up to 10 times a day; their comparatively short intestinal tract is not able to retain large amounts of food. Well-fed baby Discus fish with bulging stomachs will be 'normal' again within the hour. To maintain their health and growth, they must be fed continuously. Once they are about six to eight weeks old, and have reached a size of approximately 3 cm, the frequencies of feeding can be changed.

If baby Discus fish are neglected during the first two months of their life, they will be permanently stunted; even if they are then fed more often, and on better foods, they will never catch up and grow to their full size. Eyes that are over-large in proportion to the body are clear evidence of neglect during the first two months.

If the fish have grown normally, and are two months old their feeding schedule can be reduced to six or seven times a day. Any suitably sized food can be given, and should be eaten within a minute or two. If the fish are fed often but sparingly, they will constantly hunt for any uneaten food on the bottom of the aquarium. It may take the hobbyist a while to establish the right amount of food for a given number of fish, but giving two small portions a few minutes apart is better than giving the whole amount in one go.

By the time they have reached 6 to 7 cm, the frequency of feeding can again be reduced somewhat; at this stage it is probably less important than the quality of the food, but the growth of the Discus can still be maintained by feeding them only five or six times a day. To keep adult fish in good condition, they should be fed four times a day; when looked after in this manner, they are less likely to fall ill.

The suggested frequencies of feeding can be carried out even by a hobbyist who, because of his professional commitments, has not got much time to spare. Even though Discus fish will feed in semi-darkness, the time-switch for the aquarium lighting should be set so that the light will already have been on for at least half an hour before the first food is given in the morning. Most hobbyists will have at least one hour in the morning between getting up and leaving to go to work; during this hour, the fish can be fed twice. Members of the family can probably be persuaded to give the fish several measured amounts of food in the course of the day. On returning from work, the hobbyist once again takes over the responsibility: several more feedings are possible before bedtime. Discus fish looked after in this way will respond with a fast growth rate, general good health and willingness to spawn.

The common practice of occasionally withholding food for one day should not be carried out on fish younger than about two to three months, because it could easily affect their growing cycle. In older specimens it seems to be beneficial. After a day's fast, the water is less burdened, giving the biological flora a better chance to purify it, resulting in more alert and colourful fish.

SUITABLE FOODS

Many different kinds are available, so there is no need to give the fish a restricted diet. Many people stress the importance of giving live foods; yet they often harbour parasites and diseases which can do much harm in the warm water of the Discus aquarium. Live foods may in some ways benefit the health and well-being of the fish, but only if they are 'clean', or can be thoroughly sterilized.

BRINE SHRIMPS

Adult brine shrimps are the cleanest and safest live food available, and can be fed both to fish as small as 3 to 4 cm, and to adult fish. Nowadays these shrimps are commercially propagated, and are available on a regular basics. They will live in the water for some time, and are one of the best foods for the hobbyist to use to make his fish start feeding after they have been moved or imported.

Although brine shrimps are mostly water, without any great nutritive value, they should be given more than once a week. Adult brine shrimps are also available deep-frozen, both the white-grey variety and the reddish type from Thailand.

DAPHNIA

This is another crustacean that can be used for settling Discus fish into a new aquarium. The larger *Daphnia magna* is more easily taken than the smaller *Daphnia pulex*. Again, their nutritive value is very low, since they mostly contain water. They are often used by Discus fish breeders as an occasional laxative, especially after several feedings of a high protein diet.

Live *Daphnia* should only be fed to Discus fish if one can be sure that they were collected from 'fish-free' ponds. It is known that *Ichthyophonus* can be introduced into the aquarium with live *Daphnia*; and all fish fed with infected *Daphnia* will show the infection within weeks. *Daphnia* should therefore only be given to Discus fish if no other clean food is obtainable. *Daphnia* is also available deep-frozen, but is usually taken only by younger fish.

RED MOSQUITO LARVAE — BLOODWORMS

These small red worms are one of the best conditioning foods for Discus fish. However, live bloodworms carry a certain risk of disease and should only be given sparingly, and only to healthy fish, which are better able to cope with the introduction of certain parasites.

When live bloodworms are given, they should first be kept for several days in fresh water with a live-food sterilizing agent. The water should be changed once or twice a day and kept cool. The live worms should be put into a coarse net, suspended in a bucket of water; many of them will wriggle free, and it is only the wriggling bloodworms that should be given. Red Mosquito Larvae are also used to introduce into the fish certain medications and/or vitamins, by being soaked in them for some time. Deep-frozen Red Mosquito Larvae are always much safer and have now become the staple diet for many Discus fish.

BLACK MOSQUITO LARVAE

Black Mosquito Larvae are another good, nutritive food for Discus fish. In Europe they are available in the summer months, and can be collected by any one who has access to a pond or a pool of standing water. Even a water-butt in the back garden will collect a certain amount of these larvae during the course of the summer, but they must be fed to the fish before they have had a chance to hatch out: In Singapore, it is an offence, punishable by a very heavy fine, for anyone to cultivate Black Mosquito Larvae for live food. These small larvae are an excellent food for young fish; they are also taken by adult Discus fish, but not as keenly as by young ones. Black Mosquito Larvae are also available deep-frozen.

WHITEWORMS

These small white worms can easily be propagated by the hobbyist, using a commercially available culture. They have a very high nutritive value, and should therefore be given only once or twice a week to adult fish, but more often to growing fish. Whiteworms can also be used as carriers of vitamins. They are sometimes available as a deep-frozen food, but because they are so easy to cultivate, most hobbyists will have one or several cultures on the go.

GLASSWORMS

Glassworms, the larvae of *Chaoborus*, have a very limited season, they should certainly be given whenever they are available. They are another of the conditioning foods for Discus fish, and no fish ever refuses them. They can be kept for quite a long time, either in a bucket of water in a cold place, or in wet newspaper in a domestic fridge.

LIVE *TUBIFEX*

For years these were considered to be the chief diet for fish. Today they are known to be responsible for many mortalities in the aquarium, and should not be given, especially to Discus fish. They are collected in very polluted waters and carry a great variety of fish pathogenic organisms as well as chemicals and heavy metals. 'Clean' *Tubifex* are a very good conditioning and growth food for Discus fish, but since they are no longer safe, especially in Great Britain and Europe, their use must be discouraged.

EARTHWORMS

These are also a good conditioning food and can easily be collected; but only worms from chemically-free soil should be given to the fish. Earthworms can be cleaned, internally as well as externally, by being put through a sandbox. They are put on the bottom of a small wooden box, measuring about 15 cm x 15 cm x 30 cm (length x depth x height); the box is then filled with medium-sized gravel and water is poured over it. After a little while, the earthworms emerge at the surface; they are now cleaned. Any worm larger than 1 to 1.5 cm may have to be cut to a size suitable for feeding.

DEEP-FROZEN FOODS

Apart from the deep-frozen foods already mentioned, i.e. Brine Shrimps, Red Mosquito Larvae, and Black Mosquito Larvae, there are several other varieties which are keenly taken by Discus fish.

The eggs of the freshwater shrimp *Macrobrachium rosenbergii* are an excellent food for Discus fish up to about 10 cm. With adult fish, these eggs must be blended with oxheart. There are also small freshwater or saltwater shrimps being offered, usually as *Mysis Shrimps*.

Some of these foods will be accepted by some of the fish at certain times, while the other fish will completely ignore them. It is up to the hobbyist to make sure that his charges get enough variety; even though they may refuse a particular food when it is first given, this does not necessarily mean that this type should not be offered again. From my own experience, I can say that Discus fish can be made to eat almost anything; any new or alien food should, however, always be given as the first food of the day. The first time, it will probably be completely ignored; the second and third time, the Discus fish may be willing to try it; and on subsequent feedings it will be found that the fish are willing to take more and more. But care must be taken, in trying out new foods; only very small amounts should be given at first, since, most of it will probably have to be siphoned out again, until the fish has learnt to accept it.

FLAKE, PELLETED AND TABLET FOOD

These foods are manufactured by several companies, and are a good addition to the Discus diet. The larger flakes and pelleted foods, specially intended for cichlids, have a high protein content, and once the Discus fish have accepted this fare, they usually become very keen on it. Because of the size of the flakes and pellets, the amount can easily be controlled.

Baby Discus fish, from the age of about three weeks, should always have one or two food tablets, such as TetraTips stuck to the glass: they will make for them without fail. Bernd Degen describes in his book *Das grosse deutsche Diskusbuch*, an effective method of administering medicaments. A few food tablets are ground down and mixed with medicaments and a little water. This mixture is then smeared on to some other whole food tablets and allowed to dry overnight; the next day it is offered to the fish. Being already used to eating food tablets, they will now take the medicaments with their food, and it will then have the best possible effect.

PREPARED FOODS

There are several deep-frozen, oxheart-based, prepared foods available, but many hobbyists have their own formula. Oxheart is a cheap, clean food, and by varying the ingredients, many different kinds of food can be made out of it, so no Discus fish should ever get bored with the fare offered. Discus fish that are fed exclusively on different kinds of oxheart-based prepared foods seem actually to grow faster than fish that do not receive this kind of food.

I have used the following formula for many years, and all fish, from three weeks old babies to fully grown adults, will accept it, with only some difference in the manner of preparation. For baby Discus fish it is prepared in a liquidizer, whereas for larger fish, a mincer or food processor is used.

For 1 kg of pure oxheart the following additional ingredients are needed : 25 g of TetraRuby flake food, 50 g of Tetra DoroMin Chichlid pellets, 100 g of deep-frozen Red Mosquito Larvae, 100 g deep-frozen Black Mosquito Larvae, 100 g deep-frozen shrimp eggs, 100 g of DisciAmin Powder, 4 bottles of Aquabiofood U, a small quantity of gelatine or agar and 5 ml of Protovita multi-vitamin preparation. (This vitamin preparation has a short shelf-life and must be kept in a domestic fridge).

To obtain 1 kg of pure oxheart, approximately 2 to 2.5 kg will in fact be needed, since more than half of it will usually have to be discarded. The fresh oxheart must be freed from all fat, blood vessels and other tough fibrous matter and cut into small pieces: these are then put into a food processor and ground down with a little water until they are almost completely liquidized. The Tetra-Ruby and pre-soaked DoroMin pellets are added and thoroughly mixed in, then the DisciAmin Powder, after which it may be necessary to add a little more water. Finally, the water soluble vitamin preparation is well mixed in. All this is then divided into four equal parts. To the first

part only one bottle of Aquabiofood U is added, and the mixture is bound together with a little gelatine or agar. The second part is mixed with 100 g of deep-frozen Red Mosquito Larvae, a bottle of Aquabiofood U and a little gelatine or agar; the third part, with 100 g of shrimps eggs, a bottle of Aquabiofood U and a little gelatine or agar; and the last part with 100 g Black Mosquito Larvae, a bottle of Aquabiofood U and a little gelatine or agar. These four different mixtures are then put into plastic bags or ice-cube containers, and frozen. If ice-cube containers are used, they must be put into plastic bags, or covered with aluminium foil. When all is frozen, it is then cut into pieces the size of squares of chocolate and all mixed together.

In this way the hobbyist can obtain four different kinds of food — even though they are all based on oxheart. By using other additions, various 'flavours' can be achieved. I mix all my prepared foods together, keep them in a large plastic storage container, and feed the Discus fish with whatever part of the mix comes to hand. I do not keep the varieties separate, because I can never remember what the fish had the last time. Even if they get the same food two or three times in a row, they do not seem to mind. They respond well to this mixture, grow at a good steady rate, and show no signs of any deficiencies.

Deep-frozen foods should be given to the fish in its frozen condition. It was once suggested to me that by feeding Discus fish on frozen food, I was subjecting them to chilling of the intestine, resulting in *Spironucleus*. I cannot agree with this, having over the years fed many thousands of Discus fish on food which was still frozen. The outside of the solid food block starts to thaw as soon as it is put into the warm aquarium water, and the small amounts that the fish are able to take immediately become soft. As the food is held together with gelatine or agar, it sinks to the bottom without

disintegrating. By the time it has reached the bottom, the fish are able to pick at it. If it were allowed to defrost beforehand, much of it would be dispersed in the aquarium, most of it being lost to the fish and resulting in polluting the water.

VITAMINS

Vitamins are a food supplement, and are essential for the health and well-being of the fish. They play a vital role in the chemical reactions within the body, and a shortage of vitamins will lead to deficiency disease. The amounts required depend not only on the size of the fish, but also on the type of food being given as well as on their environmental conditions. Vitamins are needed for the proper development of the eggs and larvae, and they are needed for a sustained growth rate and the development of bone structure. Discus fish which have been given vitamins as a food supplement are also less prone to disease.

Deformed and shortened gill covers in baby Discus fish are the result of vitamin deficiency. It was thought for a long time that these deformities were hereditary, but it has now been established that they are due solely to a vitamin deficiency at an early stage of development.

The most important vitamins for Discus fish are the B-complex (B1, B2, B5, B6, B12, biotin, folic acid, nicotinic acid, pantothenic acid) and vitamin E. They must be administered in a water-soluble form, and stored below 10° C. If they are put directly into the water, this should be done when the aquarium lighting is off, because most of them are destroyed by light.

Vitamins have a greater effect if they are given mixed into prepared food, or if live foods is allowed to soak in a vitamin solution. To do this, a few vitamin drops are mixed with a little water, and the food is left to soak in this for about 10 minutes or so.

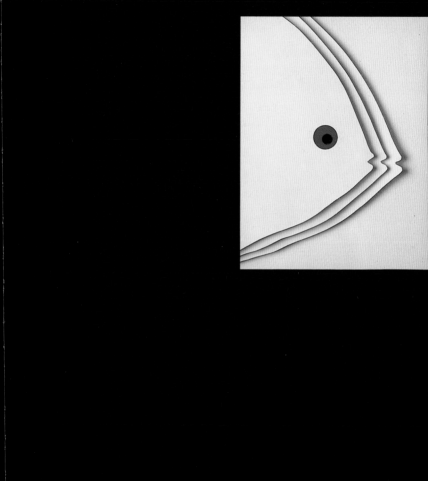

DISEASES

*DISEASE: SYMPTOMS AND TREATMENT ●
HEXAMITA/OCTOMITUS/SPIRONUCLEUS ●
COSTIA, TRICHODINA AND CHILODONELLA
● DACTYLOGYRUS ● GYRODACTYLUS ●
CAPILLARIA ● BACTERIAL GILL AND FIN
ROT ● PROTRUDING EYES AND SWOLLEN
ABDOMEN ● 'WHIRLING' DISEASE ● RED
NOSES ● HOLES IN THE HEAD ● ACIDOCIS
● GRAM NEGATIVE COLUMNARIS*

I said in my introduction to this book that of all imported Discus fish, about ten % will still be alive after three months. Why are there these tremendous losses. Basically because all the imports are diseased, most of the importers are unable to deal with many of these diseases, and finally, as a result of incorrect diagnoses by the hobbyist, wrong and completely ineffective medicaments are administered. Generally, the Discus fish die not from the actual diseases, but because of the interaction of the many drugs used.

I have regularly had many specimens of Discus imports examined, both those from South America and those from the Far East; it was found that all Discus fish were to some extent infected with many fish-pathological parasites and other diseases. Over the years, I developed a series of treatments which would guarantee that any Discus fish offered to one of my customers would be free of disease. After treatment, specimen Discus fish were once again examined, and it was found that they no longer harboured any parasites or other infections.

In principle, three different treatments were used: *Ektozon*, for the prevention and control of ectoparasites and endoparasites; *Masoten*, for the treatment of internal worm infestation of *Capillaria*, of skin flukes *Gyrodactylus*, and of gill flukes *Dactylogyrus*; and *Metronidazol*, for the treatment of Hole-in-the-Head disease, *Hexamita/Spironucleus*.

Rarely was there any need to use a broad-spectrum antibiotic. The fish were treated for a period of three weeks. *Ektozon* was used within hours of their arrival and again the following day. Five days later, the fish were kept in *Masoten* for 24 hours; this was repeated after five days. Finally, two treatments of *Metronidazol* were given. From notes kept at the time, all the fish were then found to be 'clean', and stayed 'clean'; there also was a noticeable improvement in coloration and general appearance. No damage to any of their internal organs was observed, and some of the fish were able to spawn within four weeks of the end of the treatment. One fully-grown wild-caught Royal Blue male lived for another seven years without ever contracting any other disease.

Fortunately, Discus fish do not seem to suffer from many diseases. Those that they do get can be divided into three groups: induced by environmental conditions; stress-related; caused by infection or by infestation by parasites.

Ailments which fall into the first two groups are the easiest to cure, simply by providing the fish with more suitable living conditions. Infectious or parasitic diseases are often difficult to diagnose, and an examination under a microscope may be necessary in order to determine treatment. Before carrying the treatment out, however, one should make sure that the fish's environmental conditions are all they should be. There is not much point in treating Discus fish for a gill fluke infestation following heavy breathing, if they are kept in a water which is low in oxygen or too high in carbon dioxide.

All newly-aquired Discus fish should be kept in quarantine for a least a week or two. The temperature of the water should be raised for part of this time to 35°C. Heat treatment and good water quality should be the first step in preventive medication. As the second step, the therapy described earlier can be used; or the fish can be kept for one week in a treatment of *CQD* (see Glossary) and one week in *Metronidazol*. During the treatment, a good supply of oxygen is required. If the fish are found to be healthy, they can be introduced into the aquarium with other fish.

For specific diseases, specific medicaments must often be used. Many drugs used for human therapy are also very effective in the treatment of Discus fish diseases, but because of the stringent drug laws that exist in many countries, these medicaments can only be obtained on prescription from a vet.

DISEASE: SYMPTOMS AND TREATMENT

What follows is an outline of the symptoms and treatment of the main diseases and infestations that Discus fish are known to suffer from. Any fish that shows any of these symptoms may have to be removed from the company of other fish and transferred to a hospital tank, or the whole aquarium must be treated with the appropriate medicament.

HOLE-IN-THE-HEAD DISEASE, HEXAMITA/OCTOMITUS/ SPIRONUCLEUS

SYMPTOMS: Loss of appetite, dark body-colour, keeping apart from other fish; long, stringy white faeces; initially a few white pimples in the head region, often above the eyes, turning into crater-like holes. In young Discus fish the symptoms are: rapidly progressing emaciation, pinched appearance above the eyes, rotting of fins. Flagellates (thread-like organisms of the disease) can clearly be seen in the faeces under a microscope.

THERAPY: Heat treatment at 35°C for at least 10 days, with the addition of *Metronidazol* (sold as Flagyl, Metrolyl or

Vaginyl) at 200 to 300 mg per 50 litres of water for five days. Large water change of at least one-third, and the treatment repeated. At the end of the treatment, a 50 % water change. *CQD* has also been successfully used in certain cases: 10 cc of *CQD* per 100 litres of water, repeated after three to four days. At the end of therapy, 50 % water change.

COSTIA, TRICHODINA AND CHILODONELLA

SYMPTOMS: Milky-white deposits on body and fins; these parasites also attack the gills, causing rapid breathing. Clamped fins; the fish rub themselves against hard objects.

THERAPY: A 10 to 15 minute bath in kitchen salt at 15 g per litre; the fish are then moved into fresh water, or 10 cc of *CQD* per 100 litres of water, repeated after three to four days. At the end of therapy, a 50 % water change. Or 1 g of *Agriflavine* per 100 litres of water for about 10 hours. *Agriflavine* in this concentration is very effective, but may greatly stress some Discus fish: they should therefore be watched closely, and moved into fresh water when necessary.

GILL FLUKE INFESTATION — DACTYLOGYRUS

SYMPTOMS: Choking, rapid breathing with widely opened gill covers, jerky swimming movements, rubbing against hard objects.

THERAPY: 24 hour bath in *Masoten* at 40 mg per 100 litres of water, followed by a one-third water change; treatment repeated after 8 to 10 days. As most gill flukes are egg layers and the eggs are not destroyed by any medication, it is important to repeat the treatment, in order to kill the hatched-out gill flukes. Large water change at the end of the treatment, and charcoal filtration, or *CQD*, at 10 cc per 100 litres of water, repeated after three to four days. At the end of therapy,

50 % water change.

(Please note that when using *Masoten*, handle it cautiously, and follow implicitly the instructions on the container).

Round Worm and Ichthyophonus cyst on Discus.

BODY FLUKE INFESTATION – *GYRODACTYLUS*

SYMPTOMS: Milky-white clouding of the skin and torn fins. The fish lose their colour and keep in corners. Accurate diagnosis is only possible with a microscope.

THERAPY: 24 hour bath in *Masoten* at 40 mg per 100 litres of water: usually one treatment is enough. Large water change at the end of the treatment, and charcoal filtration, or *CQD*, at 10 cc per 100 litres of water for five days; at the end of therapy, 50 % water change.

Fluke on Discus.

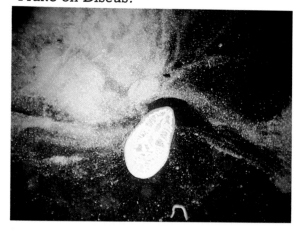

THREADWORMS – *CAPILLARIA*

SYMPTOMS: Refusal to take food, thin white faeces and slightly swollen belly. These are sure signs of infestation with *Capillaria*, but accurate diagnosis is only possible with a microscope.

THERAPY: Prolonged bath in *Masoten* at 45 mg per 100 litres of water: daily 25 % water change and the addition of 25% *Masoten* until the faeces are normal (three to six days). At the end of therapy, 50% water change, and charcoal filtration.

BACTERIAL GILL AND FIN ROT

SYMPTOMS: Initially, diseased fish show milky-white edges to both fins and gills; at an advanced stage, fins and gills are destroyed. Increase in body slime. The fins and gills, however, will in most cases grow back. Bacterial fin-rot is caused by bad water management.

The condition of this Discus fish was the result of neglect over a period of time.

THERAPY: Prolonged bath in *Chloromycetin* or *Ofloxacin* at 250 mg per 20 to 25 litres of water; dose repeated daily for at least four days. With all antibiotics, correct dosage must be used, to prevent the development of resistant strains of bacteria.

Certain antibiotics will also cause vitamin deficiency, especially of the vitamin B-complex as well as of vitamin E, which is required for fertility. During

treatment with antibiotics, additional vitamins must be administered to the fish. In the Far East, where drugs are generally available without prescription, many antibiotics are used unnecessarily, and this may be the reason for the high percentage of infertile Discus fish.

PROTRUDING EYES AND SWOLLEN ABDOMEN

SYMPTOMS: As the name suggests; they appear at a very early stage of the disease. It is usually caused by bacterial infections, due to 'old' water and inefficient filtration, and can be kept at bay by good water management.

THERAPY: 50% water change and renewal of filtering materials; 250 mg *Chloromycetin* per 20 litres of water, until the symptoms disappear.

'WHIRLING' DISEASE

SYMPTOMS: This disease seems to appear only in Discus fish from Singapore. They grow quite normally until they are about five to six months old, with no apparent signs of ill-health. At five to six months, the fish suddenly begin to dash through the aquarium, often in a circular motion. This may occur only once a day at first, becoming more frequent and more violent during the next few days. The fish will hit the sides or cover glass of the aquarium with such a force as to render itself temporarily unconscious; after several of these attacks, it will no longer regain consciousness. It is thought that an internal parasite is the cause of this behaviour.

THERAPY: To my knowledge, there is no cure. A few of these fish have seemed to be cured with heat treatment, 35°C for 8 to 10 days. Until the cause of this disease has been determined, the mortality will be high.

RED NOSES

SYMPTOMS: As the name suggests. They can clearly be seen, and are caused either by bacterial infection, or by haemorrhage.

THERAPY: If bacterial, an antibiotic should be used. *Chloromycetin* at 250 mg per 15 to 20 litres of water for three to five days will clear the symptoms. If the redness is the result of a broken blood-vessel, it will stay for a long time, but the fish seem to be able to cope with it without showing any ill-effects.

HOLES IN THE HEAD

SYMPTOMS: Again, as the name suggests. These very small holes in the region above the eyes, gills or on the face are clearly visible, and can be seen in young fish as well as in adult fish. There is no lesion from the holes as would be the case of *Hexamita*; they seem harmless and are probably the result of environmental conditions. Often these holes will disappear without therapy.

ACIDOCIS

SYMPTOMS: The fish either become very dark in colour or look very bleached. The cause is prolonged exposure to very acid water, resulting in a milky-white skin turbidity. Part of the protective mucous trails from the body of the fish, making it susceptible to disease.

THERAPY: Immediate partial water change with alkaline water over a period of time. The carbonate hardness of the water must be increased and maintained with commercially available pH adjusters. Exhausted filtering materials to be renewed.

GRAM-NEGATIVE *CULUMNARIS*

At the beginning of 1987 a new kind of disease was found to be spreading to many parts of the Discus fish keeping world. It originated in Singapore and/or Malaysia and affected only Discus fish and Angel fish. Because so many Discus fish were imported from these countries, this disease spread very rapidly. It was found in Sweden, Denmark, Germany, Austria, Great Britain and even the USA. What was so puzzling was that the Discus fish were completely normal one minute, and dead the next. Once the disease got a hold in the aquarium it spread very fast, and heavy losses were suffered by breeders, importers and hobbyists. The disease seemed to affect largely young fish only. The disease was identified at the Auburn University, NY, as Gram-negative *Culumnaris*.

Although the disease is serious, it does not necessarily affect all the Discus fish at the same rate. They may live for another two or three weeks as long as the water is not allowed to become foul through the addition of medicines. Most of the diseased fish die as a result of the fouling of the water and not because of the actual disease.

SYMPTOMS: There are none: the fish die suddenly without warning, and a post-mortem examination under a microscope is needed for diagnosis.

THERAPY: To about 100 litres of water, add 250 to 350 g of iodine-free cooking salt. If the fish suffer stress from this concentration, add more water. The mucous membrane will begin to peel off the fish giving of an extremely foul smell. After a while move the fish into clean water, adding two to three capsules of *Tetracycline*. The temperature of the water should be maintained between 32° to 33°C. Repeat treatment daily, using a little less salt each time. From the second day on, use *Agriflavine* at a concentration of about 1.5 g per 100 litres of water, instead of *Tetracycline*, but still maintain the temperature between 32° to 33°C. The fish will become clean within seven or eight days when there should be no longer any sign of skin secretion. The most important point to remember is that the fish must be moved into clean water once the salt bath has had its effect. *CQD* has also been found to be effective in combating this disease, alone or combined with an antibiotic.

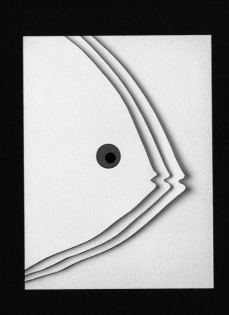

GLOSSARY

AGAR: Obtained from algae and used as a binding agent in prepared foods.

ACI-TONER: Toner substance, alkaline → neutral → acid.

ALKA-TONER: Buffer, acid → neutral → alkaline.

AEROBIC: Capable of living only in the presence of oxygen.

ANAEROBIC: Capable in living in the absence of oxygen.

ANIONS: Negatively charged ions.

AQUABIOFOOD U: Baby Discus fish food, manufactured in Germany by AB Aquatechnik.

AQUACONDIT: Water conditioner based on organic substances, manufactured in Germany by Kolbmann.

AUTOTROPHIC: Organisms capable of synthesizing complex organic substances from non-living inorganic compounds.

BIOTOPE: Clearly defined habitat with overall optimum conditions.

BROAD SPECTRUM ANTIBIOTICS: Effective against both gram-negative and gram-positive bacteria.

CATIONS: Positively charged ions.

CHLORAMPHENICOL (CHLOROMYCETIN): Broad spectrum antibiotic.

CILEX: Breeding aid and live food disinfectant, manufactured in Germany by Brustmann.

CLONT: German trade name. See → Metronidazole.

CQD: 'Come Quick Danger'. Powerful Discus fish remedy, manufactured in Germany by Kolbmann.

dH: Degree of hardness, also deutsche hardness.

DISCIAMIN: Discus fish-specific tonic containing amino acids, manufactured in Germany by Kolbmann.

DISCIAMIN POWDER: High protein food supplement and colour enhancer, manufactured in Germany by Kolbmann.

DUOLITE A303: Weak base anion exchange resin.

DYLOX: American trade name. See → Masoten.

EKTOZON: Oxygen salt, manufactured in Germany by Brustmann.

FERROGAN: Organic iron for the aquarium, manufactured in Germany by Brustmann.

FLAGYL: English trade name. See → Metronidazole.

HETEROTROPHIC: Organisms capable of obtaining organic compounds as food by feeding on other organisms.

ION: A electrically charged atom.

LEUKOMYCIN: German trade name. See → Chloramphenicol.

LEWATIT: Ion exchange resins manufactured by Bayer Chemicals.

LEWATIT S100 G1: Strongly acidic action resin.

LEWATIT M 600: Strong basic anion exchange resin for the removal of nitrate.

LEWATIT MP 62: Weak basic anion exchange resin for two-column demineralization.

MASOTEN: Dimethylester of (2,2,2,-trichloro-1-hydroxyethyl)-phosphonic acid.

METRONIDAZOLE: Effective cure for *Hexamita/Spironucleus*.

MULM: Decayed matter.

NITROBACTER & NITROSOMONAS: The principal nitrifying bacteria in biological filtration.

OFLOXACIN: Broad spectrum antibiotic.

PROTOVITA: Water soluble multivitamin preparation.

REGENERANT: Hydrochloric acid for cation exchange resin and sodium hydroxide for anion exchange resin.

TETRACYCLINE: Antibiotic consisting of a basic structure of four rings (tetracyclic).

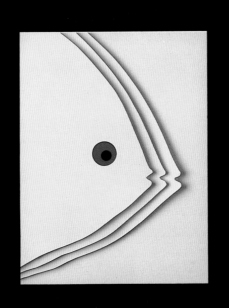

REFERENCES

AXELROD, Dr. Herbert R., *All about Discus*, (TFH Publications, Inc., Ltd., 1970, 1972).

BAYER INFORMATION, 'Die Anwendung von LEWATIT-Ionenaustauscher in der Aquaristik', (May 1968).

BLEHER, Heiko, 'Solving the Mystery of the Tefé Green Discus', *Tropical Fish Hobbyist*, (August 1986).

BURGESS, Dr. Warren E., 'New information on the species of the genus *SYMPHYSODON* with the description of a new subspecies of S.DISCUS Heckel', *Tropical Fish Hobbyist*, (March 1981).

DEGEN, Bernd, *The new German Discus Book*, Bede Verlag (November 1987).

DUIJN, C. van, *Diseases of Fishes* Iliffe Books (1973).

GEISLER, Dr. Rolf, *Wasserkunde fuer die aquaristische Praxis*, Alfred Kernen Verlag, Stuttgart (1964).

KELLER, Gunter, *Diskus*, Franckh'sche Verlagshandlung, Stuttgart (1974).

SCHMIDT-FOCKE, Dr. E., 'Color Varieties of Discus', *Tropical Fish Hobbyist*, (September 1982).

SCHMIDT-FOCKE, Dr. E., 'Vererbt sich die rote Körperfarbe bei Diskusfischen?', *Tetra Information* No 40 (December 1977).

SCHRODER, J.H., *Vererbungslehre für Aquarianer*, Franckh'sche Verlagshandlung Stuttgart (1974).

SCHULZE, Eberhard, 'Amazonas', *Aquarist & Pondkeeper*, (May 1978).

SCHULZE, Eberhard, 'Further Notes on Keeping and Breeding Discus', *Aquarist & Pondkeeper*, (May 1984).

SCHULZE, Eberhard, 'King of the Aquarium', *Today's Aquarium-Aquarium Heute*, (December 1985).

SCHULZE, Eberhard, 'Masoten, (for the contol of ectoparasites in fish)', *Aquarist & Pondkeeper*, (February 1974).

SCHULZE, Eberhard, 'The Discus Fish', *Aquarist & Pondkeeper*, (October 1974 and October 1975).

SCHULTZ, Leonard P., 'A review of the Pompadour or Discus Fishes, genus *Symphysodon* of South America', *Tropical Fish Hobbyist*, (June 1960).

SPOTTE, Stephen H., *Fish and Invertebrate Culture* (Wiley-Interscience 1970).

WATTLEY, Jack, *Handbook of Discus*, TFH Publications, Inc., Ltd., (1985).